THE WORL

First published 2008 by
Liverpool University Press
4 Cambridge Street
Liverpool L69 7ZU

British Library Cataloguing-in-Publication data
A British Library CIP record is available

ISBN 978-1-84631-165-9

Designed by March Graphic Design Studio, Liverpool
Front cover photograph by Bronek Kram
Cover images courtesy of Wilkinson Eyre Architects
Printed and bound by Gutenberg Press, Malta

THE WORLD IN ONE SCHOOL

The History and Influence of the Liverpool School of Architecture 1894–2008

Jack Dunne and Peter Richmond

LIVERPOOL
UNIVERSITY PRESS

Guangzhou Towers, China, Wilkinson Eyre. The west tower is currently under construction and due for completion in 2010. When completed it will be the tallest building in China and have the highest occupied level in the world. Here the final plan to build two towers is shown. When completed they will form a gateway to the city of Guangzhou from the Pearl River.

Wilkinson Eyre Architects

FOREWORD

The establishment of the Liverpool School of Architecture (then called the School of Architecture and the Applied Arts) under its first Roscoe Professor of Architecture, Frederick Moore Simpson (1894–1904), was an important event for the city of Liverpool and its artistic and architectural community. However, it was also to prove a significant step for the wider international design community. As David Thistlewood noted in his centenary review of the school in 1995, 'To reflect on the history of the School of Architecture is to discover a microcosm of ... twentieth-century architectural influences and values.'[1] Under Sir Charles Reilly's influence it became the first university School of Architecture to design and run RIBA accredited degrees in architecture from 1902 and the school would go on to number six Gold Medal winners among its graduates and staff, and to establish an international reputation as a centre of excellence in architectural research and education. Those influential figures who have achieved eminence in the fields of architecture, architectural education and planning include Sir James Stirling; Lord Holford; Edwin Maxwell Fry; Sir Peter Shepheard; Sir Stirrat Johnson-Marshall; Sir Patrick Abercrombie; Gordon Stephenson; and Colin Rowe. The school's architect graduates such as Herbert Rowse, Harold Dod, Frank Williamson and Maurice Lyon built many important buildings in Liverpool, but they also spread a style of architecture that became known as the 'Liverpool Manner' around the world from Johannesburg to Cairo.

The school continues to produce architects of outstanding quality and influence including Jonathan Falkingham, co-founder of the groundbreaking firm of Urban Splash and architect / director of ShedKM, which have pioneered the regeneration of the city centres of Liverpool and Manchester together with other schemes throughout the UK; Jim Eyre of the firm Wilkinson Eyre, designer of the Millennium Bridge,

Gateshead, the new Liverpool Arena and Conference Centre, as well as numerous international projects; and Jonathan Ellis-Miller, a multiple RIBA prize-winner and currently influential in the government-sponsored Building Schools for the Future programme. A healthy sign of ongoing excellence is the award of 'Young Architect of the Year', which was won in 2005 by a recent graduate, Patrick Lynch. The Liverpool School of Architecture of course remains an important part of the cultural life of the City of Liverpool and the city's outward-looking international focus is intertwined with both Liverpool University and the school's research and teaching agenda. The *World in One School* exhibition and this associated publication have been created as one of Liverpool's European Capital of Culture 2008 events. It is an exploration of the history of the school and what its teachers and graduates have achieved internationally in designing and constructing the architecture of the world. Quentin Hughes, one of the school's esteemed teachers, writing in his seminal book *Seaport* said of Liverpool 'This seaport is a world city looking out across the Atlantic, linked to the Americas and the Eastern trade, not parochial and introvert ...'[2] Like the city, those who began their architectural careers here have also proven to be neither parochial or introvert.

Professor Robert Kronenburg
Chair of Architecture
Head of School

[1] David Thistlewood, 'Liverpool School of Architecture: Centenary Review', *The Architects' Journal*, 11 May 1995, p. 60.

[2] Quentin Hughes, *Seaport: Architecture and Townscape in Liverpool*, London, Lund Humphries, 1964, p. x.

THE WORLD IN ONE SCHOOL The History and Influence of the Liverpool School of Architecture 1894–2008

THE EARLY YEARS (1894–1904)

The School of Architecture and Applied Arts, under its first Roscoe Professor of Architecture, Frederick Moore Simpson (1894–1904), admitted its first students in the Lent term of 1895, prior to its official opening on 10 May and initially concerned itself with instruction in painting, sculpture, fine plasterwork, stained glass, carpentry, ironwork and enamelling. The reputation of the school was quickly established and among the early instructors were Augustus John (1901–03), Herbert McNair (1897–1905) and Robert Anning Bell (1894–98). The school's accommodation, however, was rudimentary with staff and students working in buildings adapted as workshops that became affectionately known as the 'Art Sheds'.[1] As the school was not part of the municipalized system, its teaching programme was able to evolve outside the constraints of the South Kensington System of Instruction – the system used in the municipal colleges of art – allowing it to develop a heavy emphasis upon the then fashionable Arts and Crafts and Art Nouveau styles, as evidenced in the decorative work undertaken by students on the Philharmonic Hotel on Hope Street, Liverpool (1899–1900).

Running alongside this seam of decorative work were Simpson's own interests and sympathies with classicism and the strong classical tradition of the city of Liverpool, which had been built up via the efforts of latter-day merchant princes such as William Roscoe (1753–1831) and families such as the Rathbones and Holts, and which was manifested in buildings such as Harvey Lonsdale Elmes's St George's Hall (1841–54). Simpson's own enthusiasms for Beaux-Arts classicism can be seen in his design for the Victoria Monument, Derby Square, Liverpool (1902–06). During his time as Roscoe Professor, Simpson established links with American architectural practices and began to slowly shift the emphasis of the school away from its stylistic roots towards Beaux-Arts classicism.[2] Simpson was an admirer of both the French and American models of architectural training as evidenced in a pamphlet he published as early as 1895[3] and as Crouch notes: 'That Simpson ultimately planned a School of Architecture modelled upon the American is without doubt. His respect for the course at Columbia University is further reinforced through his acknowledgment of the receipt of "much valuable information" from its Professor, William Ware.'[4] When Simpson accepted the chair of Architecture at University College, London, it coincided with the split of the school into two sections – the Applied Arts section joined the Municipal School of Art, with Architecture remaining within the university. The concentration upon pure architectural training that had begun in the years immediately before the split (the BA honours course in Architecture began in 1900; RIBA Intermediate Exemption in 1902), allowed the new Roscoe Professor, (Sir) Charles Herbert Reilly, to build upon the work undertaken by his predecessor to establish the school on both a national and international footing.

THE REILLY YEARS (1904–33)

Reilly was just 30 years old when he was appointed Roscoe Professor; a photograph taken by Mary 'Bee' Phillips, a student in the school, shows a group of students along with Reilly and fellow instructors Charles J. Allen and James Herbert MacNair circa 1904 (fig. 1). While he possessed a first class degree in engineering from Cambridge University, experience in the offices of John Belcher and Stanley Peach, together with teaching experience from evening classes at King's College, London, he had built little and was not well known in architectural circles. Reilly quickly set about establishing himself within the newly independent university and became part of a grouping within the Arts Faculty known as the 'New Testament', which saw the university and the city in general as a new Athens at the hub of a vast mercantile empire. Commentators such as Mary Bennett have described the appointment of Reilly as a 'new phase ... bringing with him a return to the classical tradition and an enormous advancement in influence'.[5] In his autobiography, Reilly recalls himself 'at once ... putting away the Gothic casts and putting the Renaissance and classical ones into positions of greater prominence'.[6] Certainly Reilly liked to portray himself as a new classical broom sweeping away the outmoded Arts and Crafts of his predecessor and while this was not strictly the case, he was very successful in promoting this impression.[7] In contrast to Simpson, who was a gentle and scholarly aesthete, Reilly had few pretensions where scholarship was concerned. What he did possess was a strong sense of public relations, a sociable and forceful personality and a talent to seize every opportunity in order to promote himself, the school and his students in the press and professional journals. He wrote widely in a variety of publications from *Tit-Bits* to *Country Life* and was at one time Consulting Editor to the *Builders' Journal* as well as being a regular contributor to the *Architects' Journal* where, from 1926 onwards, he wrote a series of annual summaries of the previous year's buildings. He also published a handful of books, including *Scaffolding in the Sky: a semi-architectural autobiography* (1938).

The earliest attempts Reilly made to publicize the school came in the form of the *Portfolio of Measured Drawings;* the first was published in 1906, with a second edition appearing in 1908. These included studies by students of Liverpool's finest classical buildings, and helped establish the classical ethos of

Fig. 1 Staff and students of the Liverpool School of Architecture and Applied Arts. The photograph was taken by one of the students, Mary 'Bee' Phillips, circa 1904. Seated on the back row, left to right, are C. J. Allen, J. H. MacNair and the new Roscoe Professor, Charles Herbert Reilly.
Board of Trustees of the National Museums and Galleries on Merseyside: Walker Art Gallery

7

Fig. 2 St George's Hall, Liverpool:
Composition of Details from Bay of
Main Hall, Measured and Drawn by
Captain E. N. Frankland-Bell VC.

*The Liverpool University Architectural
Sketch Book, 1920*

Fig. 3 Lever Prize Competition,
Municipal Buildings, 1913, F. Jenkins.

*The Liverpool University Architectural
Sketch Book, 1920*

Fig. 4 The Athenaeum Club, Church Alley, Liverpool, Harold Dod, 1928. Harold Dod (1890–1965) was one of Reilly's early students in the Liverpool School. He joined the firm of Willink and Thicknesse and worked on the Cunard Building in the city. Dod's design is heavily influenced by the work of McKim, Mead and White and is a perfect example of the American Beaux-Arts which Reilly helped to promote through his teaching and writing from 1909 onwards.

The Book of the Liverpool School of Architecture

the school in the minds of the wider architectural community. A further series entitled *The Liverpool Architectural Sketchbook* followed in 1910, 1911, 1913 and 1920, and provide an interesting chronicle of the school's architectural stance during the middle period of his tenure (figs. 2, 3). Reilly stated in the introduction to the first edition 'in Liverpool we have … made our choice. We have determined that Monumental architecture shall be the basis of our system.'[8] Of the various examples to be found, Harold A. Dod's *Design for an Art Gallery,* from the 1911 volume, shows the school's technique at its best. Dod would go on to design a number of buildings in the school's mature Beaux-Arts, most notably the Liverpool Athenaeum Club (1924–28, fig. 4). Leonard Eaton described Dod's design as being polished and elegant in proportion: '[it] bears a strong relationship to similar buildings in New York, such as the Metropolitan Club … by McKim, Mead and White'.[9] The American influence upon the school was further strengthened by Reilly's first visit to the USA in 1909, and he returned with a suitcase full

of material he had collected from the various practices he visited. The American influence had been evident from Simpson's time at the school, and Liverpool in general was intimately connected with American commerce and trade, making the city fertile ground for Reilly's enthusiasm for American Beaux-Arts. As a reviewer of students' work from the school noted in *The Builders' Journal* of 10 July 1912:

> It is, in fact, evident that the United States furnishes either the model or the inspiration for the composition, and even detail, of nearly every essay in the design … the manners of … Charles Follen McKim, Hornbostle, Cass Gilbert and Van Buren Magonigle are the chief favourites.

Beaux-Arts appealed to Reilly on both an ideological and practical level – ideologically it appealed to his natural internationalism and dislike of a 'national' style, be it either Gothic or Arts and Crafts; or, as Crouch puts it, Beaux-Arts styling was 'a fitting symbol

Fig. 5 India Buildings, Water Street, Liverpool, Herbert J. Rowse. Rowse was the most influential Liverpool-based architect of the inter-war years, building several large office buildings of which this was the first, together with the city's concert hall. He also worked on the Queensway Tunnel, the first tunnel under the River Mersey. India Buildings was built in partnership with Briggs & Thornley. Reilly considered the building 'would not disgrace Fifth Avenue; indeed, it would sit there very happily and those who know most of modern architecture will know this is very high praise'.

Peter Richmond

representing a universalised metropolitanism'.[10] On a practical design level it allowed for Reilly's declared preference for monumental classicism to be executed in a 'readable' manner. As Crouch notes,

> What Beaux-Arts styling was able to do, in the eyes of its adherents, was to enable the construction of large buildings whose subsequent proportions were familiar enough culturally for them to be accessible, and so to become monumental in appearance, rather than incoherently large.[11]

This would be demonstrated to good effect in the work of an early graduate of the school, Herbert James Rowse (1887–1963, Cert. Arch. 1907), such as India Buildings, Water Street, Liverpool (1924, fig. 5), and Martin's Bank head office, Water Street, Liverpool (1927–32, fig. 6). Reilly led by example with his Beaux-Arts design for Devonshire House, Piccadilly, London

(1924–27, fig. 7), in collaboration with Thomas Hastings. The style was easily adapted by the teaching methods used within the school: 'The Liverpool ethos of strong abstract composition bearing informed cultural references ... led Stanley Ramsey ... to characterise Reilly's achievement as "Modernism with ancestry"'.[12]

Arguably the main achievement of the early years of Reilly's tenure was the establishment of the Department of Civic Design. This came about via a collaboration between the university and William Lever (Lord Leverhulme), the soap magnate. Reilly was tapping into a general interest in planning issues that had been current in architectural circles, both in Britain and America, throughout the latter part of the nineteenth century. This came to a head in Great Britain in the form of a speech made by John Burns, President of the Local Government Board, following promises by the new Liberal government to introduce a Bill to alleviate overcrowding. Lever had a long-established interest in architectural and planning matters, as demonstrated by

Fig. 6 Headquarters of Martin's Bank, Water Street, Liverpool, 1927–32. The second large office block designed by Rowse on Water Street. The building combines Beaux-Art massing with Egyptian and Jazz Moderne decorative detailing. Particular attention was paid by Rowse to the technical requirements of the building. It is a completely ducted office block, free of exposed pipes or wires and employs an early example of low temperature ceiling heating.

The Book of the Liverpool School of Architecture

Fig. 7 Devonshire House, Piccadilly, London. Thomas Hastings with Charles Herbert Reilly, 1924–27. Reilly was invited to propose an American architect to design an apartment block to replace the old Devonshire House. Reilly suggested his friend Thomas Hastings (1860–1929) and was appointed joint architect with him. The design was modified mid-way through, the original scheme being too large, but it remains a fine example of American Beaux-Arts Classicism in London.

Peter Richmond

Fig. 8 Scheme for the laying out of the central portion of Port Sunlight Village, Ernest Prestwich, 1909. Prestwich (1889–1977) was the first winner of an annual prize set up by William Lever (Lord Leverhulme), open to senior students of the Liverpool School of Architecture, as part of the establishment of the Department of Civic Design. The first place prize was £20 and an additional fee of £100 was to be paid if the final scheme was finally implemented. Prestwich's design – a grandly formal axial plan on Beaux-Arts lines – was finally modified and extended by James Lomax Simpson and T. H. Mawson. Prestwich was to recall, many years later, that on winning the prize he felt like a 'millionaire' and headed for Aintree racecourse, where he was 'discovered' by Reilly, who upbraided him for wasting money!

The Book of the Liverpool School of Architecture

Fig. 9 Design for Observatory and Planetarium on Bidston Hill, Fifth-Year Thesis Design, 1931, by Robert Gardner-Medwin.

University of Liverpool, Archives

12

his workers' village at Port Sunlight[13] and was enthusiastic that the department should reflect current theories on planning issues. Lever provided finance for the employment of a professor and the publication of a journal on planning – *Town Planning Review* – together with the Lever Prize which was intended to encourage high-quality planning schemes.[14] The first prize was won by Ernest Prestwich (1889–1977, BA 1910, MA 1912) (fig. 8), with a design for the planning of part of Port Sunlight. From their launch, it was the intention that both the *Town Planning Review* and the Lever Prize should comprise a forum for planning debates on a national and international level. The first professor appointed was a former colleague of Reilly's from his London days, Stanley Adshead, and he was assisted by (Sir) Patrick Abercrombie (1879–1957, MA 1912, RIBA Royal Gold Medallist 1946), the brother of a university colleague of Reilly's. From the outset Adshead and Reilly used part of Lever's funding to travel abroad to view architectural and planning schemes. As Reilly stated with his typical boldness

> It was decided that he [Adshead] and I should divide the world between us at his lordship's expense. Adshead was to travel through Europe collecting information as to what was being done in town planning in Germany, Austria and elsewhere, and I was to go to the eastern states of America and do the same.[15]

Both Reilly and Adshead gathered large amounts of material that would help inform their teaching methods along with the architectural and planning ethos of the School of Architecture and Department of Civic Design. In a report submitted to the university Senate in 1912, Reilly was able to proudly state that

> It is not too much to say that the Town Planning Review has raised the whole subject of town planning in England from the purely utilitarian point of view from which it was at first regarded, and has therefore justified the inclusion of the subject in the work of the School of Architecture.[16]

When Adshead left the department he was succeeded by his deputy, Abercrombie, who built upon the growing reputation of the department. Abercrombie would go on to have a distinguished international career as a planner, cementing Liverpool's reputation as a pace-setter in planning education, being awarded a RIBA Royal Gold Medal in 1946.[17]

Reilly established from the outset of his tenure in the Roscoe Chair a system of design education that placed a strong emphasis upon an adaptation of the Beaux-Arts system, consisting of esquisses and projects, culminating in an elaborate final design thesis. Reilly largely disliked the formal lecture system he had experienced in other institutions and preferred rather to walk around the design studios giving on-the-spot instruction. This method would be used by other schools as the core method of design instruction, largely as a consequence of graduates of Liverpool taking up prominent teaching positions elsewhere. Students' imaginations were stimulated by Reilly's innate sense of the dramatic and he would set projects for the exotic and fanciful such as 'A Queen's bedchamber', 'A Palace for Kubla Khan', or with a subject that included a dramatic physical or literary location such as 'A chapel on a rocky promontory'. Projects such as museums and observatories (fig. 9) would provide a bridge between the domestic and the institutional offering incrementally more complex planning challenges. This allowed students to build their confidence in the use of the correct application of the Orders together with the deployment of axis and vistas. This consistent design philosophy and the highly directed compositional drawing style gave Liverpool an advantage over other schools of architecture in competitions such as the Rome Prize, and under Reilly the school averaged more than four Rome Scholarship finalists each year – including the first Rome Prize winner, Harold Chalton Bradshaw[18] (1893–1943, Cert. Arch. 1913, Rome Scholar 1913).

The outbreak of the First World War saw Reilly take up a position as an Inspector of Munitions, leaving the running of the school to his deputy, Lionel Bailey Budden (1887–1956, BA 1909, MA 1910). Budden had been an outstanding student in the school and was a scholarly addition to the teaching staff. In the years immediately after the war, Budden won a series of commissions – often in collaboration with the Liverpool sculptor Herbert Tyson Smith – to design war memorials, including Birkenhead and Liverpool (1925 & 1926, fig. 10). Other graduates who designed memorials included Trenwith Wills (1891–1972, Cert. Arch. 1910) design for Hightown, Lancashire (1919); William Naseby Adams (c.1887–1952, Dip. Arch. 1908) and Eric Ross Arthur's (1898–1981, B.Arch 1922) design for Dewsbury (1923–24), as well as Reilly's County War Memorial for Durham (1928). It was in the years immediately after the war that Reilly began his major recruitment drive of overseas students. There had been a steady flow of students from the Empire and associated countries prior to 1914 as the student record cards show[19] but with the end of hostilities Reilly stepped up his efforts, partly as a means of boosting numbers to force the university to provide better accommodation[20] but principally because he wished to increase the scope and influence of the school. Between 1919 and 1932, the school attracted, on average, five or six overseas students each year.[21] A number of these students, such as George Checkley (1893–1960, Liverpool School of Architecture 1919–22), attended on ex-serviceman's grants. While not all those who entered the school on such grants stayed the course, however, those who did often went on to carve out distinguished careers and they would number among them future Professors of Architecture at schools in Canada, New Zealand and Britain. Checkley was born in New Zealand and had trained under the Christchurch architect Cecil Wood prior to serving in the New Zealand Expeditionary Forces. He went on to forge a distinguished academic career, first as a lecturer at Cambridge University, then Master of Regent Street Polytechnic School of Architecture and finally as Head of Nottingham University School of Architecture from 1937–48. Checkley was a pioneer of British Modernism and while at Cambridge he designed two early Modernist houses. Eric Ross Arthur came to Liverpool from New Zealand on a Kitchener Scholarship and would go on to work for both Sir Edwin Lutyens and Sir Aston Webb before being appointed Professor of Architecture at Toronto University in 1923. Other students were drawn from such diverse countries as Uruguay, Ceylon, Panama, Siam, Egypt, India and the USA, among others.[22]

Students also travelled in the opposite direction; for example, Frederick Williamson's work on the University of Witwatersrand, South Africa, together with various other domestic and commercial commissions, and Maurice Lyon's (BA 1906) Post and Telegraph Office in Cairo (fig. 11), both display the 'Liverpool Manner' – a term coined by Randall Phillips to describe the school's brand of classicism[23] – of monumental classicism on an imperialist scale. Other graduates, however, made attempts to respond to the traditional architecture of the country. Philip Cape Harris (Cert. Arch 1910), who worked as Government Architect in Zanzibar throughout the 1920s, used an Islamic style in his additions to the Sultan's palace, also in his design for a Maternity Clinic in Zanzibar (1925, fig. 12). Harold Clayforth Mason (1892–1960, Cert. Arch. 1911) used Middle Eastern models for his St George's Church in Baghdad – regarded by Freya Stark as one of only two good buildings erected by the British in Iraq[24] – while his design for Basrah Airport from (1937, fig. 13), in collaboration with Cyril A. Farey, relied heavily upon

Fig. 10 War Memorial, Hamilton Square, Birkenhead, 1925, Lionel Bailey Budden (1887–1956). Budden designed a number of war memorials including winning the competition design for Liverpool's Cenotaph. He worked with the sculptor Herbert Tyson Smith on the design for this and the Liverpool memorial. Students had produced earlier alternative designs for this memorial in 1919 (see *The Liverpool University Architectural Sketch Book*, 1920, p.61).

The Book of the Liverpool School of Architecture

Fig. 11 Egyptian State Telegraph building, Cairo, 1927, Maurice Lyon. Maurice Lyon was one of the students Reilly had 'inherited' from his predecessor, Professor Simpson. Lyon's design was exhibited at the Royal Academy in 1927 and is a typical example of the monumental classicism which became known as the 'Liverpool Manner', for which the Liverpool School of Architecture became famous in the inter-war years. Graduates of the school exported the style to all corners of the British Empire and beyond.

The Book of the Liverpool School of Architecture

Fig. 12 Maternity Clinic, Zanzibar, 1925, Philip Cape Harris. Harris was Government Architect in Zanzibar from 1922 until the early 1930s. In addition to this design he made several additions and alterations to the Sultan's Palace which also attempted to use a style sympathetic to the original building and the vernacular architecture of Zanzibar.

University of Liverpool, Archives

Fig. 13 Basrah Airport, 1937, Harold Clayforth Mason (architect),
Cyril A. Farey (1888–1954, perspectivist). Mason brought this
commission with him when he left the post of Government Architect
in Iraq and entered into partnership with J. M. Wilson in London,
1935. The airport was designed to accommodate both flying boats
and conventional aircraft. It incorporated an hotel and restaurants
alongside the usual terminal facilities. It was one of the first fully air-
conditioned buildings in Iraq.

Wilson Mason and Partners, Chartered Architects, London

Fig. 14 Church of St Andrew and Hospice, Jerusalem, 1925–26, Albert Clifford Holliday. Holliday was Civic Adviser to the City of Jerusalem from 1922 and then Town Planning Advisor to the Palestine Government from 1926, combining the posts with private practice in Jerusalem. Holliday's design draws upon his knowledge of the city's historic architecture and uses traditional materials combined with elements that are noticeably modern.

The Book of the Liverpool School of Architecture

Fig. 15 House for Mogul Bay Fathy, Pyramid Road, Giza, c.1930s, Aly Labib Gabr.

University of Liverpool, Archives

Fig. 16 Apartment House, Cairo, c.1930s, Aly Labib Gabr.

University of Liverpool, Archives

European Modernism which was seen as being an international style by its proponents. Robert Pearce Steel Hubbard (1910–65, B.Arch. 1932, Rome Scholar 1932) and Albert Clifford Holliday (1897–1960, Dip. Civic Design 1920, B.Arch. 1922) managed to combine European Modernism with aspects of local architectural tradition in their work in Palestine. Holliday's Church of St Andrew and Hospice, Jerusalem (1925–26) illustrates this approach, using as it does traditional materials combined with modern elements (fig. 14). Their work together on banks for Barclays, such as the branch in Jerusalem in 1930, incorporated mild historicist detailing befitting its setting, while the branch in Haifa (c.1935), built of concrete cast in situ, is more starkly cubic Modernist in conception. A block of apartments and shops they designed for central Haifa in 1937 was featured in a display of work of past students of the school held at RIBA in May 1937, where Reilly considered them to be the outstanding exhibit.[25] Reilly stated of Hubbard's work in Malta that he was 'possibly the best man we have … to design simple modern buildings yet in sympathy with the Baroque architecture for which Malta is famous'.[26]

While the Liverpool School was establishing an international reputation, a further reason for its success was the limited opportunities for architectural training within the British Empire. In 1920, Liverpool and the Architectural Association were the first schools to have their five-year courses accepted in lieu of the final examinations for Associateship of the RIBA. A few schools would follow – McGill University, Montreal in 1923 and a handful more in South Africa, New Zealand and Australia – but even by 1937 there were no schools in Asia or the Middle East offering exemption. The consequence was that nascent architects in Empire countries looked to the British schools for their training and few were as well known as Liverpool under Reilly. A further factor was Liverpool's central position as a great trading port and many students were attracted from non-Empire countries including those in North and South America, with occasional students from Norway, France, Holland, Spain, Belgium and Iceland, through family trade connections. The flow of students was often prompted by graduates of the school gaining positions of authority in other countries leading to closer ties with Liverpool. For example, during Maurice Lyon's period as Government Architect in the Ministry of Works in Cairo during the 1920s a succession of Egyptian students chose to study in Liverpool, a pattern repeated when Harold Clayforth Mason was Government Architect in Iraq.

With the return to England of Harold Clayforth Mason and Maurice Lyon in the 1930s, the pattern of British-born, Liverpool-trained architects exporting the Liverpool style to Iraq and Egypt came to an end. Rather, Liverpool-trained, native-born architects, such as Ahmed Mukhtar (Dip. Arch. 1936), who was appointed Government Architect in Baghdad in 1938, and Mohamed El Hakim, who worked for the Ministry of Endowments in Cairo from 1934–49, took up key posts. Some would combine their Beaux-Arts stylistic training with elements of the vernacular architecture of the region, such as Aly Labib Gabr's (B.Arch. 1924) designs for houses in Cairo (figs. 15, 16). Mohammed Makiya, who was born in Iraq and came to Liverpool in 1936, recalled that he brought little knowledge of Middle Eastern architecture with him. Makiya would return to Iraq as a teacher of architecture; here he 'exported' his Liverpool training in measured drawings and used it in his own teaching syllabus in an attempt to stimulate his students' interest in vernacular architecture.[27] Nai Saroj Subhung (Cert. Arch. 1918, Dip. Arch., Dip. Civic Design 1920) returned to Thailand – then called Siam – and was put in charge of all the country's temples. Two Egyptian graduates, Mahmoud Riad (B.Arch. 1931) and Mahomet el Hakeem, worked extensively in

19

Fig. 17 A Combined Bus and Railway Terminal Station for Alexandria (perspective drawing of concourse), Fifth-Year Thesis Design, 1920s, Mahmoud Riad.

University of Liverpool, Archives

their home country as well as building a mosque in Athens. As with Makiya, Riad's thesis design for a Combined Bus and Railway Terminal for Alexandria (fig. 17) owes more to his Western Beaux-Arts training than any understanding of his native Middle-Eastern tradition. Nevertheless, the influence of the 'Liverpool Manner' and Western architectural training had a strong influence upon the work produced, in many cases overwhelming the local traditions. Such examples of cultural imperialism may seem at odds with our modern sensibilities; however, they were not an issue for the generation in question. As Sharples notes, 'By 1935 Reilly could write, apparently without irony, how strange it was "that with the variety of climates and races included in the Empire, so few buildings with local characteristics are put up ..."'[28]

Women students were present from the earliest days of the school, albeit in small numbers. Reilly was encouraging in terms of admitting women and indeed his daughter studied briefly in the school before leaving the course to marry former graduate and

studio instructor in the school, Derek Lawley Bridgwater (1899–1983, B.Arch. 1924). There are a number of surviving examples of work by women who studied in the school; for example, Constance Stammers' fifth-year thesis design for the British Industries Fair, Birmingham, a monumental modernist conception (fig. 18), and Miss Miles's (Mrs Solomon) fourth-year design for a Monument to the Founding of the United States of Europe from 1929 (fig. 19). Reilly was realistic enough to acknowledge that the male-dominated profession would mean that many women would struggle to establish themselves in anything more than supporting roles as assistants in the larger practices.[29] However, there were exceptions; Norah Dunphy (B.Arch. & Cert. Civic Design 1926) became a Town Planning Assistant to Tynemouth and North Shields Corporation in 1931, making her the first woman to hold such a post.[30] Frances T. Silcock (Dip. Arch. 1925) married a student contemporary and went into practice with him, and Josephine Reynolds (Dip. Civic Design 1944, MA 1953) was a lecturer in the

Fig. 18 Design for British Industries Fair, Birmingham, Fifth-Year Thesis Design, c.1930, Constance Stammers.

University of Liverpool, Archives

Fig. 19 Monument to the Founding of the United States of Europe, Fourth-Year Design, 1929, Miss Miles (Mrs Solomon). The subject of the design is typical of the sort of subject Reilly liked to set his students. It reflects his internationalist outlook while setting the students a topic upon which they could develop their creative skills.

University of Liverpool, Archives

Fig. 20 A Skyscraper Tower, 1929/30, Alwyn Sheppard Fidler. Reilly was very much excited by the sight of the New York skyscrapers he saw lit up at night: 'To see brilliant windows and towers of light floating in the sky, where ordinarily one expects to see stars, means that one treads the pavement in no solemn, downcast manner. One walks on air, not knowing what to expect' (Charles Reilly, *Some Architectural Problems of Today*, 1924, pp.175–76). Reilly particularly liked the classically dressed New York skyscrapers and he would encourage his students to produce designs in this manner, a number of which were illustrated in the *Liverpool University Sketch Books*.

British Architectural Library Drawings Collection / Royal Institute of British Architects

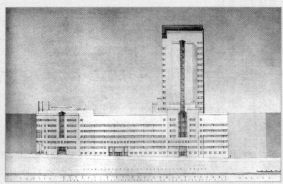

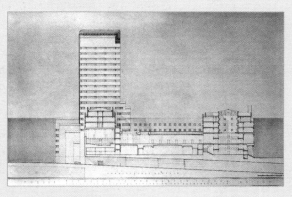

Figs. 21, 22 Proposed Municipal Buildings and entrance to Mersey Tunnels, Fifth-Year Thesis Design, 1931, Norman Sykes Lunn. When the Old Haymarket was proposed as the site for the new Mersey Tunnel, c.1926–27, the opportunity arose to combine the tunnel entrance with a new civic building. Lunn's design – two towers with a linking building spanning the tunnel entrance – gives some idea of what might have been achieved. Reilly later said that he had suggested to the Tunnel Committee that Lunn's design might be a possible solution (*Liverpool Review*, August 1934, pp.273–75). Lunn had spent his fourth year in the New York offices of Corbett, Harrison and MacMurray and the detailing of his thesis design shows clear references to the Art Deco skyscrapers he saw there.

The Book of the Liverpool School of Architecture

Fig. 23 City of the Future, 1931, Edwin Maxwell Fry. This was published as part of the development plans of New York in the 1931 *Regional Plan of New York and its Environs*, (Vol. 2: The Building of the City, p.152). Fry had spent the summer vacation of his fourth year in the New York offices of Carrere and Hastings and it might well have been through contacts made then that he was to receive the commission for this drawing. The 'City of Towers' was then very much part of the common currency of modernist architects who looked to Le Corbusier for their inspiration.

Avery Architectural and Fine Arts Library, Columbia University in the City of New York

Department of Civic Design. All too often, however, the student record cards note only that a female student had graduated and married, with no further mention of career activity.

Throughout the 1920s and early 1930s the teaching methods and design philosophy within the school was evolving from the monumental classicism developed prior to 1914, taking on influences from Europe and America. Reilly had long used contacts in the USA to place his students for office practice. In 1920 three students spent their summer break working in the New York offices of various architectural firms. Some graduates worked on prestigious projects such as Gordon Stephenson's work on drawing out and rendering the presentation plan of Corbett, Harrison and MacMurray's first, unexecuted, design for the Rockefeller Center; Edwin Maxwell Fry (1899–1987, B.Arch. 1923) was employed on one of the Long Island mansions designed by Carrere and Hastings; and George Kenyon (1908–76, Dip. Arch. 1930) was employed by Shreve, Lamb and Harmon on the elevations of the Empire State Building. Others had

more mundane tasks to perform – William Holford was set to work correcting working drawings in the offices of Voorhees, Gmelin and Walker. Students such as Alwyn Sheppard Fidler (1909–90, Rome Scholar 1933) and Norman Sykes Lunn (1908–92, B.Arch.1931) reflected both Reilly's enthusiasm for New York skyscraper design and their own American work experience in student designs such as Fidler's Skyscraper Tower (1929/30, fig. 20), Lunn's Proposed Municipal Buildings and entrance to Mersey Tunnel from 1931[31] (figs. 21, 22) and Maxwell Fry's, City of the Future design (1931, fig. 23), which was published as part of the *Regional Plan of New York and its Environs*. Other students from the 1920s worked in European practices such as Chalmers Henry Hutton (1905–95, Cert. Arch. 1921, B.Arch. 1923) who worked in Paris with C. Mewes in the late 1920s. Hutton went on to work in the offices of Charles Holden and was involved in the design of a number of London Underground stations such as Osterley and Arnos Grove as well as London University's Senate House, for which he did all the detailing.

Some graduates would choose to work further in North America, notably Edward William Martin (1891–1977, B.Arch. 1922) who while having been born in Scotland, had been brought up in Delaware and before entering the Liverpool School had partial training at the University of Pennsylvannia. Martin worked a good deal for Pierre S. Dupont, together with other rich private clients, designing Colonial Revival style houses such as the Raskob House, Wilmington, Delaware (1930, fig. 24). Of his public commissions he designed the Delaware State Legislative Building, Dover (1932) and the US Post Office, Court House and Custom House, Wilmington (1935). Eric Ross Arthur (1898–1981, B.Arch 1922), built numerous houses in Canada, such as at Bayview, Toronto (fig. 25). Some commentators have questioned the relevance of such experience to ordinary practice in Britain. However, as Sharples notes 'Big American offices offered a foretaste of the large architects' departments within municipal authorities and public bodies where many of Reilly's students would later work.' John Henry Forshaw (1895–1973, B.Arch. 1922, Cert. Civic Design 1924) had worked in the New York offices of Flagg and Chambers, and would later go on to head the architectural department of the Miners' Welfare Committee and compared its division into project-based teams to the organization of a large American office.[32] As Sharples goes on to state: 'whatever practical lessons Reilly's students may have learned in New York, these placements were above all a way of fuelling their ambition by putting them at the architectural centre of the world's most prosperous, confident and technologically advanced society'.[33]

With the Wall Street Crash in 1929, opportunities for Liverpool students to study in America came to an end. While not every student had had the opportunity to work and travel abroad prior to 1929, the closure of this valuable source of work experience meant that Reilly had to look closer to home for placements. A valuable source of 'second-hand' American experience could be found in the offices of Herbert Rowse who was developing a reputation as the most important Liverpool architect of the inter-war years. His designs for India Buildings and Martin's Bank Headquarters displayed his own American experiences and influences and it was partly due to Reilly's influence that a fellow graduate of the school, Joseph Stanley Allen (B.Arch. 1922), was encouraged to return from America where he had worked in Philadelphia and New York to assist Rowse on the India Building scheme of 1924–28.[34] Allen would go on to develop a distinguished academic career starting at Liverpool University and was subsequently appointed head of the Leeds School of Architecture in 1933, and Professor of Town and Country Planning at Durham University in 1945. Rowse also provided employment for other graduates, including Donald Bradshaw and George Kenyon, whose Liverpool training, concentrating as it did upon fine draughtsmanship and classical detailing, meant that they fitted seamlessly into the working practices of Rowse's office. Alwyn Edward Rice's (1909–79, B.Arch 1933) final-year thesis design for a Concert Hall for Commutation Row (fig. 26) bears a striking resemblance to Rowse's final design for the new Philharmonic Hall, Liverpool (1936–39, fig. 27). We can only speculate as to how much input Rice had in Rowse's design during the time he spent working in his office following graduation. The move away from Rowse's former American Beaux-Arts preference towards a more streamlined modernism with Art Deco touches, also with American influence, can be traced in his work from 1931 onwards, when he was appointed architect to the Mersey Tunnel Joint Committee. The designs he produced for the entrances and ventilation shafts (fig. 28) have elegant detailing, demonstrating Rowse's ability to produce structures that are at once both functional and aesthetically pleasing.[35] When Gropius visited Liverpool in May 1934 he was taken on a tour through the tunnel and praised the interior with its functional dado of black glass framed in stainless steel.[36]

Fig. 24 Raskob House, Wilmington, Delaware, 1930, Edward William Martin. Martin had been partly trained in the University of Pennsylvania before coming to Liverpool. Following his graduation from the Liverpool School in 1922, he returned to the United States and set up practice in Wilmington. He specialized in designing houses in the Colonial Revival style of which this is one of the grandest.

The University of Liverpool, Archives

Fig. 25 House at Bayview, Toronto, Canada, 1920s, Eric Ross Arthur. Arthur graduated from Liverpool in 1923, having come to study there from his native New Zealand in 1919. In 1923 he was appointed Professor of Architecture at Toronto University where he worked extensively in the fields of Canadian architectural history and conservation.

The Book of the Liverpool School of Architecture

Fig. 26 Design for a Concert Hall, Commutation Row, Liverpool, Fifth-Year Thesis Design, 1932–33, Alwyn Edward Rice. The burning down of the old Philharmonic Concert Hall on Hope Street, Liverpool coincided with the exhibiting of Rice's thesis designs and consequently his work received a good deal of extra attention in the local press (*Liverpool Post and Mercury*, 11 July 1933). Rice went on to work in Herbert J. Rowse's offices in the early 1930s. Rowse won the commission to design the new concert hall for the Philharmonic. We can only speculate as to how much input Rice's thesis design had upon Rowse's final design and indeed to what extent he was involved in the designing of the new building. However, the massing of the exterior and arrangement of the auditorium in Rowse's design are remarkably similar to Rice's thesis design.

The University of Liverpool, Archives

Fig. 27 Philharmonic Hall, Hope Street, Liverpool, 1936–39, Herbert J. Rowse. The destruction by fire of John Cunningham's Philharmonic Hall of 1846–49 provided Rowse with the opportunity to design a hall using the latest acoustic technology. The design he produced has obvious references to the work of Dudok, with its blocked starkly cubic massing. The building contains fine Art Deco detailing in the auditorium and reception areas.

Chris Belledonne

Fig. 28 Mersey Tunnel (Queensway) George's Dock Ventilation and Control Station, 1934, Herbert J. Rowse. Rowse was called in late to provide the architectural work on the Mersey Tunnel – a move that Reilly was highly critical of, considering it a mistake not to have had an architect involved from the start. Rowse rejected his earlier preferences for a American Beaux Arts treatment and instead opted for a smooth Art Deco style, again with obvious American influences. This tower and the one in North John Street were faced in Portland stone in order to blend in with other buildings in the business district, while the others were built of brick. The building was badly damaged during the war and was largely rebuilt by Rowse between 1951 and 1952.

Chris Belledonne

27

Fig. 29 Royal Assurance Exchange Building, 1927, Harold Dod. This tall Portland stone office building is typical of the refined Beaux Arts work of Dod in the 1920s.

The University of Liverpool, Library

Other graduates, who like Rowse, remained in Liverpool and built in the 'Liverpool Manner', include an early graduate, Harold Alfred Dod (BA 1909, MA 1910). Dod joined the Liverpool practice of Willink and Thicknesse to work on the Cunard Building (1914), with the firm becoming Willink and Dod in 1920. Apart from the aforementioned Athenaeum building, Dod also designed offices for the Royal Exchange Assurance Building in the Liverpool Beaux-Arts style (1927, fig. 29). His later work for the university included the Derby and Rathbone Halls of Residence in Mossley Hill and the Harold Cohen Library on Ashton Street (1936–38, figs. 30, 31) all displaying a stripped classical emphasis derived from his Liverpool training but modified by Modernist influences. Ernest Gee (Cert. Arch. 1908), following graduation, spent a short time in Paris and Rome, before returning to Liverpool and going into partnership with Edgar Quiggin. The practice undertook a good deal of work across Merseyside and North Wales including housing on Muirhead Avenue, Liverpool, in the 1920s (fig. 32). Reilly saw the influence of Stanley Adshead in the handling of this type of neo-Georgian public housing in the inter-war years.

> I trace, as is indeed obvious, a great deal of the new standard of small house design in the better post-war housing schemes to the work of Adshead and Ramsey at Kennington, Dormanstown and elsewhere … I think it may safely be said, for instance, that the adoption in such buildings of the Georgian sash window, and its alteration from the long mansion form to the square cottage proportion, was due to them. Indeed they may claim to have ensured for the working man some of the civilities of Georgian architecture in place of the rusticities to which romantic good-natured people would have condemned them.[37]

Public and social housing would be a recurring interest among graduates of the school throughout the inter-

Fig. 30 Harold Cohen Library, Ashton Street, Liverpool University, 1936–38. Dod, like his counterpart Rowse, moved away from the Beaux Arts classicism of his early work in the 1920s, towards a version of 'Modernism with ancestry'. The front elevation is a somewhat compromised attempt to marry modernism with stripped classicism. The rear elevation is a much more convincing statement with its clearly articulated arrangement of the book stacks, laid out on eight decks.

The University of Liverpool, Library

Fig. 31 Rear elevation, Harold Cohen Library, Ashton Street, Liverpool University, 1936–38, Harold Dod.

Chris Belledonne

Fig. 32 Housing, Muirhead Avenue, Liverpool, 1920s, Edgar Quiggin & Ernest Gee. Reilly identified the influence of Stanley Adshead in this type of neo-Georgian public housing, of which the Housing Department of Liverpool Corporation built considerable amounts in the inter-war years.

The Book of the Liverpool School of Architecture

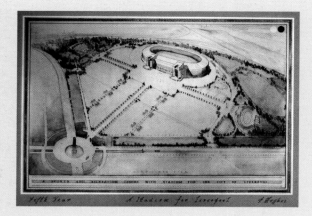

Fig. 33 A Stadium for Liverpool, Fifth-Year Thesis Design, 1931, John Hughes. This design was exhibited at the Olympic Art Exhibition in 1932, where it won a Gold Medal. The design bears some similarities to the work he would undertake as assistant to the Director of Housing (Sir) Lancelot Keay on the large tenement blocks built in the city during the 1930s.

The University of Liverpool, Archives

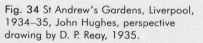

Fig. 34 St Andrew's Gardens, Liverpool, 1934–35, John Hughes, perspective drawing by D. P. Reay, 1935.

City of Liverpool Libraries and Information Service, Liverpool Record Office

Fig. 35 St Andrew's Gardens, Liverpool, 1934–35, John Hughes, perspective drawing by Leonard Berger, 1934.

City of Liverpool Libraries and Information Service, Liverpool Record Office

war and post-war period, with a number involved in the re-housing schemes undertaken within the city and beyond. Notable among these was John Hughes (1903–77, B.Arch. 1931) whose final-year thesis design, A Stadium for Liverpool (fig. 33) was awarded a gold medal at the Olympic Art Exhibition, Los Angeles in 1932. Hughes was appointed Assistant to Lancelot Keay, the Liverpool City Council Director of Housing, in 1931 and worked on the large slum clearance schemes in the city centre such as St Andrew's Gardens (figs. 34, 35, 36). He was appointed Deputy Director of Housing at Manchester City Council in 1938 and then Director of Housing, City of Westminster in 1946. Hughes's final post was as principal architect to the Ministry of Housing and Local Government for Wales, where he remained until his retirement in 1963. In the 1940s and 1950s the city architects' posts of Birmingham, Manchester, Newcastle and Southampton would all be filled by Liverpool-trained men – A. G. Sheppard Fidler; Leonard Howitt (Cert. Arch 1922, B.Arch 1925); George Kenyon (Dip. Arch 1930) and Leonard Berger.

Harold Hinchliffe Davies (Liverpool School 1919–20) along with his father Harold Edward Davies, specialized

Fig. 36 St Andrew's Gardens, Liverpool, 1934–35, John Hughes. Hughes was taken on as an assistant to Keay in August 1931, in Liverpool Corporation's Housing Department. He produced a design for a semicircular block of flats for Regent Road, Liverpool, which remained unbuilt. However, he used the same form in the north block of St Andrew's Gardens. The inspiration for the design is drawn from the so-called Horseshoe Estate at Britz by Bruno Taut and Martin Wagner. When Gropius visited Liverpool and briefly taught at the school, he was taken on a tour of the development which was still under construction. He expressed admiration for the horizontal emphasis of the windows but remarked that higher tower blocks, with more open space around them, would have been a better solution. (Liverpool Daily Post, 19 May 1934)

City of Liverpool Libraries and Information Services, Liverpool Record Office

in the design of refined classically inspired public houses
such as the remodelling of the Blackburn Arms, Catherine
Street, Liverpool, and their Jazz Moderne Clock Inn,
London Road (fig. 37). Others such as H. S. Silcock
(B.Arch 1924) worked for the city from 1925 to 1928,
designing the neo-Georgian Police and Fire Stations and
adjoining housing at Allerton. Herbert Thearle (1903–71,
Dip. Arch. 1925) had been an articled clerk in the firm of
Briggs & Thornley before enrolling in the school. He won
the Jarvis Studentship and studied in Rome in 1926. In
the same year he won the competition for the Williamson
Art Gallery, Birkenhead, designed in the Liverpool
classical manner, in collaboration with L. G. Hannaford,
and taught in the school from 1930. The partnership of
Charles Anthony Minoprio (1900–88, B.Arch. 1925, MA
1928) and Hugh Greville Spencely (1900–83, B.Arch.
1926, Dip. Civic Design 1928), while working mainly in
London and the South East, together with planning
schemes for Kuwait and Baghdad, did build a
distinguished building in Liverpool in the form of the
extension to the School for the Blind of 1930–32
(fig. 38). Designed in full-blown stripped classical style,
Reilly was so impressed by the building that he described
it as 'strong and good and fresh and modern with
interesting details – indeed with all the things one wants
and so rarely finds'.[38]

Distinguished students from the latter part of the
1920s and early 1930s included Gordon Stephenson
(B.Arch. 1930). Stephenson spent time in the New York
offices of Corbett, Harrison & McMurray and then won
the Chadwick Trust Scholarship allowing him two years
study at the Institut d'Urbanisme, University of Paris and
work in the office of Le Corbusier. On his return to
Liverpool he taught briefly in the school and in 1932
won the H. W. Williams Scholarship which promoted
design in concrete, with his Design for a Silk Factory.
The design was much influenced by Le Corbusier.
Stephenson held a Fellowship in the Massachusetts
Institute of Technology from 1936–38 before returning to

Fig. 37 The Clock Inn, London Road, Liverpool,
c.1930, Harold Hinchliffe Davies.
The Book of the Liverpool School of Architecture

Fig. 38 Extension to the School for the Blind, Hardman Street, Liverpool, 1931, Charles Anthony Minoprio & Hugh Greville Spencely. The commission for this building apparently came via Spencely's bank manager who was also the Honorary Treasurer of the School for the Blind (H. G. Spencely autobiographical notes, Walker Art Gallery Archive). The site had previously been occupied by the church of the school. The design follows contemporaneous American designs where classicism isn't abandoned entirely, but rather stripped away in order to emphasize the cubic shape. Despite this emphasis upon smooth surfaces, sculptural decoration plays an important part in the design. John Skeaping's stone reliefs illustrating the crafts practised by blind people – such as piano playing, brush making etc. – helps to soften the overall design. Reilly was especially enthusiastic about the final building considering it to be 'fresh and modern with interesting details'.

Chris Belledonne

33

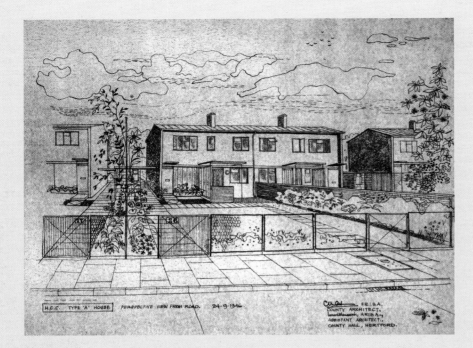

Fig. 39 Design for 'Type A' low-cost housing showing semi-detached houses with gardens, 1946, Stirrat Johnson-Marshall, Charles Herbert Aslin, Leonard Manasseh, Hertfordshire Architects Department.

RIBA Library Drawings Collection

Britain to take up a post in the nascent Ministry of Town and Country Planning during the Second World War, followed by work on Stevenage New Town. In 1948 Stephenson was appointed Lever Professor of Civic Design – designing the new building for the department. He subsequently held chairs at the Universities of Toronto and Western Australia, undertaking major city planning schemes. A contemporary of Stephenson was William Graham (Lord) Holford (1907–75, B.Arch. 1930, Rome Prize 1930). Holford was born in Johannesburg, South Africa and had been attracted to Liverpool to study by the international reputation Reilly had helped to build. After his studentship in Rome he returned to Liverpool, first to work within the school, and then in 1936 he was appointed Lever Professor of Civic Design. Holford went on to carve a highly distinguished career as a planning consultant with schemes including Team Valley industrial estate, Newcastle-upon-Tyne, and the precinct of St Paul's Cathedral.

(Sir) Stirrat Johnson-Marshall[39] (1912–81, B.Arch. 1935) had a highly distinguished career, initially as county architect for Hertfordshire from 1946 where he was responsible for the design of low-cost housing schemes (fig. 39). He subsequently worked as the Ministry of Education's chief architect from 1948, where he directed the development of a low-cost, modular prefabricated system which as Thistlewood puts it '... would resolve into near-bespoke buildings through close architect-client collaboration. The resulting schools deliberately signify little beyond their modernity ...'[40] (fig. 40).

Reilly had fostered from his earliest days in the school a strong sense of community, both within the school itself and through contacts he established in the cultural and civic circles within the city. Group photographs were taken of each student year within the school (fig. 41). The establishment of the annual Architects' Ball gave the opportunity for students to

Fig. 40 Hertfordshire County Council, School Design, 1940s, Stirrat Johnson-Marshall.
RIBA Library Drawings Collection

Fig. 41 Liverpool School of Architecture, group photograph of staff and students, 1928–29.
The University of Liverpool, Archives

School of Architecture   1928-29

design decorations (figs. 42, 43). As Myles Wright noted of these occasions, 'The Architects' Ball at the Blue Coat School was one of the biggest events of the year for the School of Architecture ... the architectural students put on a floor-show in which Reilly quite frequently appeared as an emperor or in some similar such role.'[41] Students were also encouraged to design street decorations such as Lawrence Wright's (1906–83, B.Arch. 1929, MA 1934) designs for the visit of King George V and Queen Mary, on the occasion of the celebration of the opening of the Gladstone Dock in 1927 (fig. 44) and Holford and Stephenson's designs for the Liverpool-Manchester Railway Centenary Celebrations in 1930 (figs. 45, 46). While such activities might seem frivolous and essentially ephemeral, they nevertheless encapsulate the spirit of the school in the 1920s and 1930s. The annual exhibition of students' work was also an opportunity for

Figs. 42, 43 Reilly and students in fancy dress, c.1930.
The University of Liverpool, Archives

Fig. 44 Winning design by Lawrence Wright (third year student) for the decoration of Castle Street, carried out for the visit of King George V and Queen Mary, 1927.

The Book of the Liverpool School of Architecture

Figs. 45, 46 Decorations designed by William Holford and Gordon Stephenson to celebrate Liverpool's Railway Centenary, 1930.

The University of Liverpool, Archives

SCHOOL OF ARCHITECTURE
EXHIBITION
ADMISSION FREE

Fourth Year   *L. Wright*

Fig. 47 Poster design for the annual Liverpool School of Architecture Student Exhibition, Lawrence Wright, 1928. The building depicted in the poster being exploded would appear to be Professor Frederick Moore Simpson (architect) and Charles John Allen's (sculptor) Queen Victoria Monument, Derby Square, Liverpool (1902–06). This may well have been a comment on the feeling among the students regarding the Beaux-Arts which was the favoured style of Reilly and the School of Architecture at this time. Alternately, it may well have been a comment on Reilly's known disdain for Simpson's design. Reilly described the dome as being 'half on and half off its columns' and thought it 'a pity that so much fine modelling has been expended on such a poorly placed and poorly conceived whole' (Charles Reilly, *Some Liverpool Streets and Buildings in 1921*, 1921, p.32).
The University of Liverpool, Archives

students to design posters to publicize the event (fig. 47). The sense of community fostered by Reilly would be remembered by his ex-students and colleagues for the rest of their professional careers.

Despite a long-standing offer on the part of Lord Leverhulme to provide a new building for the School of Architecture, it would not be until after Reilly's retirement that a replacement for the 'cowsheds' was finally achieved. Reilly did, however, have a hand in its design, collaborating with Budden and another former graduate James Ernest Marshall (B.Arch. 1922). The

three had collaborated already on the Veterinary Hospital at Liverpool University (1926–28, fig. 48) and would later design an extension (1935) to Reilly's 1909–14 Liverpool students' union building. The School of Architecture design defers in scale and choice of material to the early nineteenth-century merchant house to which it formed an extension, while also being recognizably modern with its long horizontal fenestration (figs. 49, 50). As Thistlewood noted, it 'respected the Georgian horizontal banding while reversing its positive and negative rhythm, thus

Fig. 48 Veterinary Hospital, Liverpool University, Charles Reilly, Lionel Budden & J. E. Marshall, 1929. The first of a trio of buildings Reilly, Budden and Marshall designed for the university in a stripped classical / modernist hybrid style.

The Book of the Liverpool School of Architecture

Fig. 49 Leverhulme Building, School of Architecture, Liverpool University, 1933, Reilly, Budden, Marshall. The purpose-built school Lord Leverhulme had promised the university before the war was finally realized by his son, the second Viscount Leverhulme, in 1933 – ironically the year that Reilly retired. The building forms an extension to one of the Georgian houses on Abercromby Square, and while recognizably Modernist in conception, Reilly et al. have paid close attention to achieving harmony between the new and the old.

The Book of the Liverpool School of Architecture

Fig. 50 Leverhulme Building, School of Architecture, Liverpool University, 1933 (courtyard).

The Book of the Liverpool School of Architecture

carrying the Reillian principle of "Modernism with ancestry" to a succeeding generation.'[42] The courtyard was originally conceived to have a Greek Doric column placed in the centre which according to Robert Gardner-Medwin (B.Arch. 1931 Dip. Civic Design 1932, Rome Scholar 1932) 'mischievously celebrated Reilly's devotion to the classical orders during the famous "cowshed" days of his reign'[43] (fig. 51).

When, due to ill health, Reilly was forced to take early retirement in 1933, the tributes paid to him illustrate the lasting debt and affection many of his students and colleagues felt. The production of *The Book of the Liverpool School of Architecture*, published in 1932, encapsulates the work undertaken by students and graduates of the school ranging from the Beaux-Arts classicism of the early years, to the emerging Art Deco modernism of the late 1920s. Reilly would only truly embrace Modernism in the full sense following his retirement, but as Stanley Ramsey noted in the essay he wrote as a tribute to Reilly

He is at the present moment with Professor Budden and his other colleagues initiating (or perhaps I should say has initiated – I prefer to keep to terms of relativity) what purports to be a very important ... contribution to 'Modern' architecture ... the beginning of a new epoch ... Behind these fresh and sometimes startling presentations of designs for modern buildings, is the quiet force of a traditional culture ... the new modern note at Liverpool ... is modern with a difference ... It is, if I may so phrase it, 'Modernism with Ancestry' ...[44]

Even after his retiremen, Reilly continued to use his influence and contacts to help secure work for graduates of the Liverpool School. It was through his recommendation that William Crabtree (1905–91, Dip. Arch. 1929) came to be appointed as a research assistant by the John Lewis Partnership. Crabtree worked briefly under Joseph Emberton where he was the perspectivist on a design for the New Empire Hall, Olympia, London (c.1929, fig. 52). Reilly had sent Crabtree's 1929 final-year thesis design for a department store to Spendan Lewis, owner of the John Lewis chain, who was so impressed he paid for Crabtree to travel in Europe to gather information on modern department store designs as part of his plans to rebuild

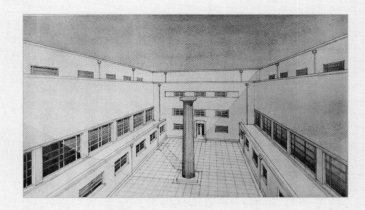

Fig. 51 Leverhulme Building, School of Architecture, Liverpool University, 1933, (drawing showing classical column) The column was never installed into the finished building.

The Book of the Liverpool School of Architecture

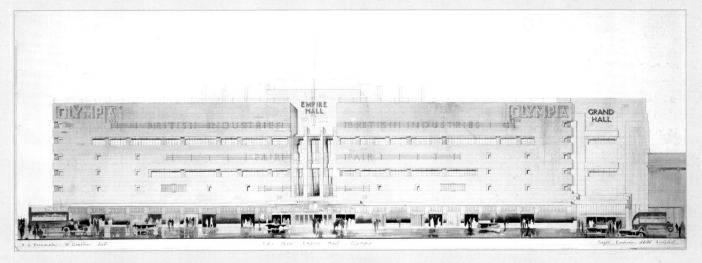

Fig. 52 New Empire Hall, Olympia, London, c.1929, Joseph Emberton (architect), William Crabtree (perspectivist).

RIBA Library Drawings Collection

Fig. 53 Peter Jones department store, Sloane Square, London, 1935–39, William Crabtree, Charles Reilly, Slater & Moberly. The building was erected in stages between 1936 and 1939. The concrete encased steel frame design and the steel and glass façade were partly a response to the European Modernism Crabtree had studied during a research trip paid for by Spendan Lewis – owner of the John Lewis retail chain – and partly due to the fact that costs for a traditional masonry structure had become prohibitive in the depression days of the early 1930s. Surprisingly, given the boldness of the design, it was an instant success and is one of the seminal buildings of early British Modernism.

British Architectural Photograph Library / Royal Institute of British Architects

the Peter Jones store in Sloane Square. The result of this research was that a design team was formed comprising Reilly as consultant architect, Crabtree, Slater and Moberly as joint architects. The design they produced and built from 1935–39 (fig. 53) is now regarded as one of the finest examples of early British Modernism. William Curtis ranks it alongside Owen Williams's Boots Factory (1930–32) as 'Two of the most remarkable buildings of the Modern movement in Britain.'[45] Crabtree went on to teach at the AA in the mid-1930s, was a member of MARS (Modern Architectural Research Group) and worked on various post-war planning schemes for Southampton and Plymouth as well as housing designs for the New Towns of Crawley, Hatfield and Harlow.

Reilly was instrumental in gaining the commission for Francis Xavier Velarde (1897–1960, Dip. Arch. 1924) to design St Gabriel's, Blackburn, 1932–33. Perhaps Reilly's most important 'placement', had it materialized, would have been the fulfilment of his desire to see Velarde take over from Sir Edwin Lutyens to oversee the completion of Liverpool's Catholic Cathedral. Reilly was a friend of Lutyens, having travelled with him in India in 1927–28. When Lutyens died in 1944, Reilly called upon Archbishop Downey's previous promise to allow him to put forward a 'continuator'. Downey kept his promise; however, it seems Velarde was unwilling to accept and the post went instead to Adrian Gilbert Scott.[46] Velarde and his fellow Liverpool graduate Bernard Alexander Miller (1894–1960, Cert. Arch 1914, B.Arch 1928) designed a number of distinguished churches in Liverpool and the north of England. In addition to his Church of St Gabriel, Blackburn, Velarde also designed St Matthew's, Clubmoor, in 1930 (fig. 54), a design which displays at its best his use of Byzantine Romanesque detail in a bold and unhesitating manner. He also designed the Church of St Monica, Bootle in 1936 with its distinctive windows inspired by the work of the German architect Dominikus Bohm (fig. 55). Sir Nikolaus Pevsner described Velarde's St Gabriel's as 'One of the milestones in the (late) development of English church architecture towards a twentieth-century style.'[47] Miller's work includes St Columba's, Anfield,

Fig. 54 St Matthew's Church, Clubmoor, Liverpool, 1930, Francis Xavier Velarde.

The Book of the Liverpool School of Architecture

Fig. 55 Church of St Monica, Bootle, 1936, Francis Xavier Velarde.

Chris Belledonne

and St Christopher's, Norris Green (1930–32), both in Liverpool. Velarde and Miller taught part-time in the school well into the post-Second World War years, acting as a 'bridge' between the Reilly, Budden and Gardner-Medwin eras. Naim Aslan (B.Arch. 1938) had worked with the Public Works Department in Baghdad before entering the school in 1932 – he would go on to collaborate with Reilly on his *Outline Plan for the County Borough of Birkenhead* which was published in 1947. Other students from this generation distinguished themselves in allied fields to architecture. Christian Barman (1898–1980, Cert. Arch. 1918) was editor of both the *Architectural Review* and the *Architects' Journal*, worked as a freelance industrial designer and produced a number of innovative designs for electrical appliances for HMV in the 1930s (fig. 56). His later career saw him work as publicity officer to London Passenger Transport, GWR and the British Transport Commission.[48] Lawrence Wright developed a career as a perspectivist, showing drawings of other architects' work in the Royal Academy Summer Exhibitions. In the 1930s and 1940s he made a number of animated films under the pseudonym Lance White, including a satire on Hitler entitled *Adolf's Busy Day* and *The Life and Career of Archie Teck*.

Reilly was Vice-President of RIBA in 1931, was awarded the Royal Gold Medal for Architecture in 1943 and knighted in 1944. The impact he had upon the Liverpool School is difficult to overstate. While Reilly's personality was complex and somewhat contradictory, what he did possess was an understanding of the power of publicity and good public relations, which was far ahead of most of his contemporaries, allied to a sociable and 'clubbable' manner. It was via these skills that he was able to promote the school and establish for it an international reputation based upon the quality of its teaching. William Holford – arguably Reilly's most illustrious student – writing after Reilly's death, noted of his former friend and professor, that he was

An international figure, not only by reputation but by the building up of personal contacts ... Reilly made himself synonymous with the Liverpool School of Architecture, but acknowledged in a much more realistic way than most that art has no frontiers. He drew his students from all walks of life and from nearly all the countries of the world ... Nor was his interest given only to his students ... with the migration ... of architects and painters and actors ... who were unable to live under the changing regime in their own countries. Reilly gave them hospitality ... recognised their integrity ... helped them with introductions and commissions ...[49]

LIONEL BUDDEN (1933–52) AND THE POLISH SCHOOL OF ARCHITECTURE (1942–45)

With Reilly's retirement the question of his successor naturally came into question. A number of the European émigrés were invited to give lectures at the school including Walter Gropius and Erich Mendelsohn, who taught for three weeks at the end of 1933 following his arrival in England. Robert Gardner-Medwin noted that

Lionel Budden ... Becoming increasingly aware of the strength of the Modern Movement ... promoted, with Reilly's blessing, the idea of inviting Walter Gropius, hounded out of Germany by Hitler ... to become Head of the Liverpool School. This would undoubtedly have transformed the school, and might well have re-awakened the fellowship of architects, designers, artists and craftsmen ... infusing it with the new Bauhaus spirit.[50]

Gropius declined the invitation and took up an offer from Harvard instead. There had been an ideological shift in the latter years of Reilly's period which

Fig. 56 HMV Controlled Heat Iron, c.1936, Christian Barman. This design was the first thermostatically controlled iron to be successful in Britain. It was not only technologically innovative, Barman's design was also highly original with the body and handle formed in one piece and moulded to fit the hand comfortably – a thumb rest on either side making it suitable for both left- and right-handed users. The design illustrates well Barman's admiration for 'the tradition of straightforward, honest, reticent design … nothing but sound sense and absolutely first class taste applied to the problem before you. Not a style, in other words, but *style* pure and simple' (*Architectural Review*, July 1933, p.13). Barman designed several other items for HMV including a fan heater c.1935. Instead of the traditional approach of an electric heater masquerading as a traditional solid fuel burner, Barman instead chose to design the fire on practical lines, with a curved front that spread the heat widely. He noted that 'I simply refuse to believe that it is necessary for electricity to masquerade as coal, gas or candles, or to gate crash into our houses cleverly disguised as these' (*Architectural Review*, October 1933, p.186).

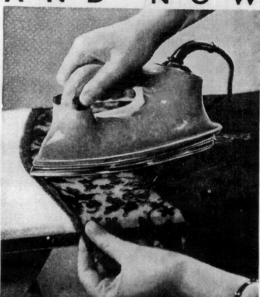

1600

1900

1935

AND NOW

The H.M.V. CONTROLLED HEAT IRON

—a departure, an iron designed for ironing by electricity. Heat controlled by the turn of a knob. Heat maintained at safe and correct temperatures, in other words—heat under control. Porcelain top in delicate primrose shade—handle designed by a sculptor.

H.M.V. HOUSEHOLD APPLIANCES LTD
363 OXFORD STREET, LONDON, W.1

continued through into the Budden era. The classical preferences of Reilly were gradually shaded into the Modernism of Budden, exemplified by the new School of Architecture building. While the full-blown Modernism of the European visiting lecturers was not perceived, at the time, as being compatible with the Beaux-Arts axial symmetry of the school's training methods, a definite shift was taking place. (Sir) Peter Shepheard (1913–2002, B.Arch. 1936; President ILA 1965; President RIBA 1969–70) noted that this seemed to have been driven by the students themselves: 'We threw away our watercolours and started going to Germany to do line drawings'.[51] Shepheard's own final-year thesis was of a block of flats that displays the heavy influence of European Modernism, particularly that of Le Corbusier.

While it might seem convenient to portray the move between the Beaux-Arts and Modernist ethos in the school as being that of a dramatic split, in essence the Beaux-Arts training methods that Reilly had set in place were perfectly suited to adaption to Modernism. As Anthony Jackson notes, 'The aspiring modern architect with a Beaux-Arts training, wishing to obey Le Corbusier's exhortations, had no need to change his method but only his formula.'[52] Wesley Dougill

recognized this when he reviewed the Liverpool School's end of year show in 1932, remarking that

> much of the success of the Liverpool School depends on the thorough grounding in traditional forms which the students receive in the earlier years of the course. It is not until they have reached the latter half of the third year that their work is preponderatingly modern. Thus there is a virtual absence of half-baked designs carried out in a style which at once presupposes a scientific and advanced knowledge of construction and materials ... which junior students cannot possibly have attained.[53]

This was perfectly illustrated by the work of Edwin Maxwell Fry. His early practice is evocative of the work of Lutyens with its combination of English Renaissance detailing and Arts and Crafts butterfly plan as in Ridge End, Virginia Water (c.1928, figs. 57, 58). Within a few years his work would seem to have been transformed as in the Sun House design of 1935 (fig. 59) – with its reinforced concrete, glass, metal, slender columns and ribbon fenestration, it is an essay in European Modernism. Kensal House (1937, fig. 60), contains an integral shop, workshop, nursery and common rooms.

Fig. 58 Ridge End, Wentworth, Virginia Water, c.1928, Edwin Maxwell Fry (entrance).

The Book of the Liverpool School of Architecture

Fig. 59 The Sun House, Frognal Way, Hampstead, London, 1935, Edwin Maxwell Fry. The shift in Fry's approach in the intervening years from the design of Ridge End demonstrates his personal architectural evolution to dramatic effect. Here Fry produces a seminal piece of British Modernism that looks not to English or American models for its inspiration but to the European work of Le Corbusier, Gropius and van der Rohe.

British Architectural Library Photograph Collection / Royal Institute of British Architects

Fig. 60 Kensal House, Ladbroke Grove, London, 1937, Edwin Maxwell Fry. Fry worked as part of a team on this project – including Elizabeth Denby, Robert Atkinson and George Grey Wornum.

British Architectural Library Photograph Collection / Royal Institute of British Architects

Fig. 61 Impington Village College, Impington, 1936, Edwin Maxwell Fry & Walter Gropius.

British Architectural Library Photograph Collection / Royal Institute of British Architects

Fig. 62 Sugar Refinery for Messrs Manbre and Garton Limited, Liverpool c.1930s, Herbert J. Rowse.

The Book of the Liverpool School of Architecture

Fig. 63 Silent House: Exhibition, Olympia, London, 1931, Arthur Trystan Edwards.

The Book of the Liverpool School of Architecture

Fry had a brief partnership with Gropius when they worked on the Impington Village College (1936, fig. 61), described as 'an essay in rational planning, organising the functions of a multipurpose educational building according to the phasing of activities during the working day and their different requirements of light and orientation – in other words, unsurprisingly, offering more than a hint of Bauhaus functional determinism'.[54] Fry's own 'conversion' to Modernism, according to his own account, took place while standing in front of Devonshire House, Piccadilly, London, during the course of its construction in 1925. Reilly designed this large Beaux-Arts apartment block in collaboration with the New York firm of Carrere and Hastings and it represents one of the finest examples of American Beaux-Arts to be found in the city. Fry recounted many years later, that he

> stood contemplating over the hoardings the rising volume of the new Devonshire House, Piccadilly, The steel framework had been standing there for some time in sufficient elegance, and what I saw now was a crust of stonework ... being hung and bolted and jointed on to the framework like so much scenery. Broad but flat-cut Florentine rustications ... were joining in an elaborate cornice, with over it a freize of fat cherubs ... Memories of New York and the school established their provenance. I knew it all like a game played out, and in those duplicating amorini, the last of their long line, I thought to find the cherubic face of my naughty professor playing Ariel to old man Hastings in New York and turned in moral revulsion from everything I had been taught.[55]

An examination of Fry's output in the late 1920s shows that his conversion to Modernism was not quite the Pauline one he describes. Fry went on to be a founder member of MARS and his subsequent career places him at the centre of British Modernism up until the 1970s. We can nevertheless see how the architectural tide was changing in the minds of young graduates of the school during this time.

Other graduates were showing similar shifts in their design philosophy, away from their Beaux-Arts roots. In Liverpool, Herbert Rowse had made his reputation as the designer of a number of large Beaux-Arts office blocks in the city's business district. By the early 1930s, his style was evolving as he embraced stripped classicism such as in his designs for a sugar refinery for Messrs. Manbre & Garton Ltd, Liverpool (fig. 62). The church and school architecture of Velarde and Bernard Alexander Miller (1894–1960, Cert. Arch. 1914, B.Arch. 1928) display an eclectic mix of inspiration from Early Christian, Romanesque and Rennaisance as well as modern German church architecture. Velarde's School of Our Lady of Lourdes, Southport (1935–36 staircase added 1952), shows obvious 'quotations' from Gropius and Meyer's Model Factory at the Deutscher Werkbund Exhibition, Cologne, 1914. An example, as Thistlewood puts it, 'of ... homage long before it became "legitimised" in Post-Modernist theory'.[56] The 1931 'Silent House' design by Arthur Trystan Edwards (Cert. Civic Design 1913) for the Exhibition, Olympia, London (fig. 63), demonstrates a similar move to that of Rowse towards a modernism derived from Dudokian sources.[57] The office of Joseph Emberton became an important source of employment for graduates from the late Reilly and early Budden years. Crabtree worked with Emberton on the design for a New Empire Hall, Olympia, London in 1929, with Philip Freeman (B.Arch. 1929) on the Royal Corinthian Yacht Club (1930–31) before going on to work with Grey Wornum on the RIBA headquarters building. John Bernard Shaw (Dip. Arch. 1935) and William Moffett (B.Arch. 1937) both assisted Emberton on the New Casino and Pleasure Beach, Blackpool, 1939. Rolf Jensen (B.Arch.

Fig. 64 White House, Conduit Head Road, Cambridge, 1930–32, George Checkley. Following graduation Checkley taught at Cambridge University where he designed a small cluster of Modernist houses for himself and other Cambridge dons around Conduit Head Road in the early 1930s.

The Book of the Liverpool School of Architecture

1933) assisted Wells Coates and David Pleydell-Bouverie with their Sunspan House and MARS Group exhibitions at Olympia, 1934. These graduates display in their work '... the classical preferences of Reilly shaded into the modernism of Budden'.[58] George Checkley designed two important early British Modernist houses in Cambridge while teaching at the university – White House at Conduit Head Road (1930–32, fig. 64) and Thurso (1932, fig. 65).

Budden, like Reilly before him, continued to befriend refugee architects from Europe forced out of their homelands by the rise of Nazism – including Ernest Wiesner, a distinguished modernist who had been architect to President Benes of Czechoslovakia. In 1942, the British Council approached the University of Liverpool with a scheme to set up a Polish School of Architecture in Liverpool and to offer sanctuary to a group of architects from Poland. Among the group were Professor Bolek Szmidt of Warsaw and Wroclau Universities, together with a young graduate teacher Lucjan Pietka and a small band of students wishing to complete their studies. The Polish School was inaugurated by the Prime Minister of Poland and Commander-in-Chief, General Wladyslaw Sikorski (fig. 66) at a ceremony held in the Philharmonic Hall on 6 November 1942 (the school had actually been in operation within the Liverpool School from June 1941). From the outset the curriculum of the Polish School was based on that of the Liverpool School but with some adjustments to take into account Polish building regulations and standards. The central aim was to produce architects who could return to Poland and help rebuild it after liberation.[59] Staff and students worked on theoretical schemes, such as for the

Fig. 65 Thurso, Conduit Head Road, Cambridge, 1932, George Checkley. Designed for Checkley's university colleague, Professor Hamilton McCombie, Thurso was built shortly after the home he designed for himself in 1930. Both houses are of concrete frame and rendered brick construction.

British Architectural Library Photograph Collection / Royal Institute of British Architects

Fig. 66 Visit of General Wladyslaw Sikorski – Prime Minister and Commander-in-Chief of Poland – on the occasion of his visit to Liverpool to inaugurate the Polish School of Architecture, November 1942. From left to right are Mr Z. Dmochowski, General Sikorski, Lieut-Col L. Torun (Director of the Polish School of Architecture), Mr L. Pietka.

The University of Liverpool, Archive

rebuilding of a specified Polish village. Other projects included designs for hospitals, a Broadcasting Centre (fig. 67), blocks of flats (fig. 68), churches and town halls as well as replanning schemes for Liverpool's Castle Street (fig. 69). Staff from the Liverpool School, including Budden, Marshall, Velarde, Miller and Thearle, worked alongside their Polish colleagues and as Boleslaw Szmidt noted of these collaborative teaching methods, they

> proved to be a most successful way of exchanging ideas on professional problems, as by this method the subject is considered from various points of view and thus a balanced judgment is achieved. In this way each programme of an architectural exercise, after being worked out by the students, is the subject of a criticism-lecture delivered ... by the British or Polish lecturers. In this respect a very important task carried out by the Teaching Staff of the Polish School of Architecture should be mentioned. It consists of a thorough study of the methods of training employed in the Liverpool School of Architecture.[60]

The emphasis on teaching Polish architectural history and the incorporation of the tradition of Baroque style and decoration in their designs resulted in a hybridization of Liverpool Modernism and Polish historicity. As well as the differences between the Liverpool and Polish methods, there were also similarities, notably the use by both of the weekly three-hour sketch design exercise. In the Introduction to a book published in 1945 to commemorate the disbanding of the Polish School following the end of the war, Budden noted that

> ... the work shown in the present volume is in the main stream of contemporary architectural thought and practice, it is yet distinctively expressive and national in character. The forms employed are in the main familiar, but they are given an unmistakably Polish inflexion – and the result is the more interesting and vigorous for that

Fig. 68 Block of Flats, Czeslaw Sztajer, Polish School of Architecture, 1944.

The University of Liverpool, Archive

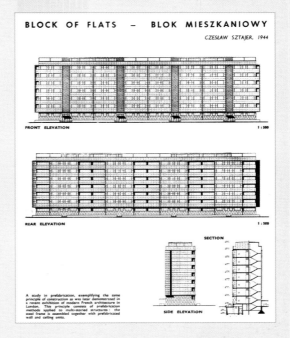

Fig. 69 Plan for the Castle Street Precinct in Liverpool, Fourth-Year Design, Polish School of Architecture, 1944, Stanislaw Lacki.

The University of Liverpool, Archive

53

reason ... From the opportunities of collaboration that have been afforded us we have learnt much. There has been a fruitful exchange of ideas between the two schools and our students have in particular appreciated the stimulus they have received from the participation of their Polish contemporaries in those sketch designs in which the latter notably excel ... We look forward therefore to the ties ... being maintained and strengthened in the days that lie ahead.[61]

The brief period of the Polish School at Liverpool would therefore seem to have proved to have been a productive one for both parties. Astragal, writing in the *Architectural Journal*, stated that

So far as I am concerned, all arguments about which is the best school of architecture in this country to-day have been settled. If the work of the students, rather than their number, is to be the criterion, the Polish School of Architecture ... at Liverpool, is hands down the winner ... It is obvious however, that such a high standard among students can only be the result of sound and imaginative teaching ... and of a wealthy reserve of architectural tradition upon which to draw.[62]

The experience of the collaboration with the Polish School may well have helped confirm for Budden the unacceptability of moving too far away from inherited forms and instead the need to maintain something of the Liverpool tradition of 'modernism with ancestry' in the teaching of the school in the immediate post-war period. Students graduating immediately after the war would go on to establish careers that would see them build major projects around the world. Among them was Vernon Lee (B.Arch. 1947, Dip. Civic Design 1948). Lee's student thesis design 'A Fine Arts Faculty, University of York' (fig. 70) shows signs of the work he

would go on to produce for the Hertfordshire Schools' Programme as well as major hospital commissions in Grenada, Trinidad, Anguilla, Belize and Glendon Hospital, Montserrat, West Indies (1970s), which was opened by Princess Anne, but unfortunately fell victim to a volcanic eruption and is now covered in ash (fig. 71). His career continued with work as Chairman of the British Consultants Bureau in 1980–82 and as Chairman of RMJM (Scotland) in 1985, before his retirement in 1989.

It was in the early years of the war that one of Liverpool's most famous graduates first entered the school. (Sir) James Frazer Stirling (Dip. Arch. 1950), completed his first year in 1941 before being called up to serve in the army, returning in 1947 to complete his course. While his time in the school overlapped only slightly with the Polish School, on his return to study he would have found the curriculum deeply infused with Polish values together with a continuing presence of a few Polish staff and students who had remained in Liverpool following the formal end of the Polish School in 1945. Stirling's final-year thesis design – a project to replace the heart of the ancient market town of Newton Aycliffe in County Durham (figs. 72, 73) with a single monolithic structure combining various building functions within a unified complex – 'only really makes sense in relation to a "Polish" expectation that the field of architectural engagement would have been totally despoiled'. Stirling's other main sources of inspiration during his student days were the city of Liverpool itself and Le Corbusier. As Rob MacDonald (BA 1973, B.Arch. 1976, PhD 1983) notes of this period in the school,

Eclecticism was the rule and modernism was only one of the options. Le Corbusier was still regarded with suspicion by members of the faculty ... the Polish School ... occupied one of the studios and its staff were all committed modernists. They were

Fig. 70 A Fine Arts Faculty, University of York, Fifth-Year Thesis Design, 1947, Vernon Lee.
The University of Liverpool, Archive

Fig. 71 Glendon Hospital, Montserrat, West Indies, 1970s, Vernon Lee.
Royal Commission on the Ancient and Historical Monuments of Scotland, Archive

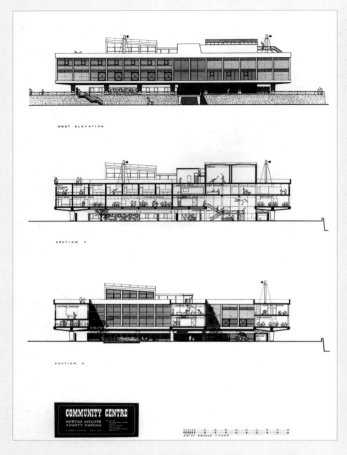

Fig. 72 Design for a Community Centre,
Newton Aycliffe, 1950, James Stirling.

The University of Liverpool, Archive

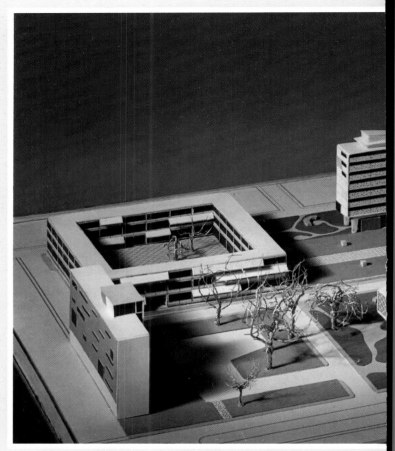

Fig. 73 Model of a Design for a Community
Centre, Newton Aycliffe, 1950, James Stirling.

The University of Liverpool, Archive

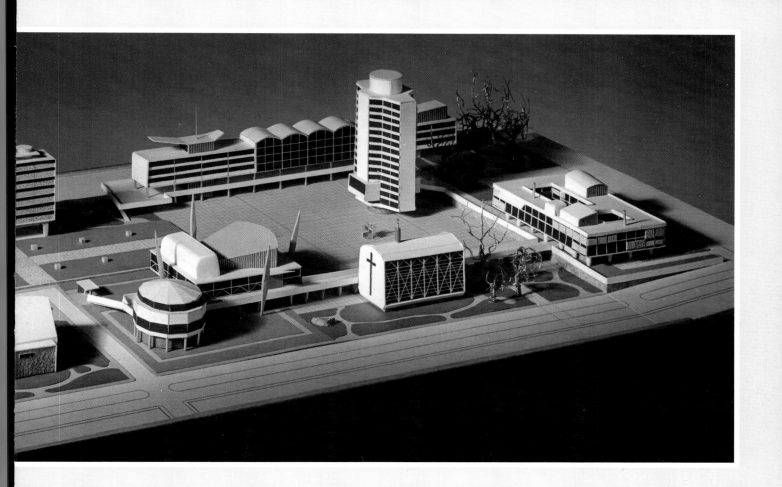

Fig. 74 Leicester University Engineering Faculty, 1959, James Stirling. Undertaken in collaboration with James Gowan, the building has large areas of glazing that contrast with the heavy masonry forms. The building was in strong contrast with contemporaneous British buildings, and forms the basis of Stirling's subsequent international career.

Neil Jackson

precise draughtsmen producing minimalist black line drawings, derived from Le Corbusier. Jim bought a book of their work and he was certainly influenced by their drawings.[63]

As his former partner Michael Wilford notes of Stirling's own drawing technique, he was 'a magician who could perform a design with a few strokes of his pencil ... we communicated all our ideas through the medium of drawing ...'[64]

The generation of students which included Stirling and Robert Maxwell and who were taught by Colin Rowe (1920–99, B.Arch. 1945, Royal Gold Medal for Architecture 1995) found the curriculum of the school at this time bland and restrictive – as an alternative, Stirling drew upon the architectural stock of Liverpool and Le Corbusier for his inspiration. Stirling would later note that the Beaux-Arts system, upon which much of the teaching of the school was still founded,

together with the Bauhaus – both systems based on pedagogic practice – 'are for us now equally unfortunate. There surely must be another way driving down between them.'[65] Much of Stirling's subsequent work can be interpreted as this 'middle way' via his quoting of admired Modernists such as in his Leicester University Engineering Faculty of 1959 (fig. 74); the Florey Building, Queen's College, Oxford (1966–71, fig. 75); the History Faculty Library at Cambridge University (1964–67) and the unrestrained historicism of the Staatsgalerie, Stuttgart (1977–84, figs. 76, 77), a design which Thistlewood describes as being 'interpretable as a sustained, beneficial effect of the Polish communitarian spirit and strong sense of responsibility towards a deeply-rooted culture'. In 1979, Stirling was commissioned to design an extension to Harvard University's Fogg Museum (figs. 78, 79, 80). The resulting design – the Sackler Museum – was not actually built until 1985 and is an

Fig. 75 Florey Building, Queen's College, Oxford, 1966–71, James Stirling.

Neil Jackson

Fig. 76 Staatsgalerie Museum, Stuttgart, 1977–84, James Stirling.

Andre Brown

Fig. 77 Staatsgalerie Museum (interior), Stuttgart, 1977–84, James Stirling.

Andre Brown

Fig. 78 Sackler Museum, Fogg Museum, Harvard University, Cambridge MA, USA, 1985, James Stirling.

Robert Kronenburg

Fig. 79 Sackler Museum (interior), Fogg Museum, Harvard University, Cambridge MA, USA, 1985, James Stirling.

Robert Kronenburg

Fig. 80 Sackler Museum (interior), Fogg Museum, Harvard University, Cambridge MA, USA, 1985, James Stirling.

Robert Kronenburg

Fig. 81 Clore Gallery, London, 1980–87. James Stirling. This was Stirling's first important project in London. From the exterior, the heightened colours and the building's relationship to the landscape form a striking contrast with the original 1897 Portland stone Tate buildings.

Neil Jackson

Fig. 82 Mfantsipim School, Ghana,
1953, Edwin Maxwell Fry & Jane Drew.
*British Architectural Photograph Library /
Royal Institute of British Architects*

independent building located across the street from the Fogg. The exterior is striped orange and grey brick, with the colour scheme continued in the interior – the use of colour would be a motif of Stirling's work from this period, repeated in other commissions such as his design for the Clore Gallery, London (fig. 81), reflecting his belief that architecture is an expression of art and not merely a product of social planning and engineering. Stirling established an international reputation, working on major commissions around the globe, and being awarded the RIBA Royal Gold Medal in 1980 and the Pritzer Prize in 1981. He was an honorary member of the Akademie der Kunste in Berlin and the American Institute of Architects, and was knighted shortly before his premature death in 1992. The annual British national architecture award, the 'Stirling Prize', is named in his honour, reflecting the enormous influence he had upon the national and international architectural scene.

ROBERT GARDNER-MEDWIN (1952–73)

Following Budden's retirement in 1952, Robert Gardner-Medwin was appointed to the Roscoe Chair. He had been a student in the school in the Reilly era and returned to Liverpool after a distinguished career as an architect-planner, working in the West Indies as well as for the United Nations Mission to South East Asia and the Department of Health in Edinburgh. The experience Gardner-Medwin gained in his work overseas would help to inform his stewardship of the Roscoe Chair. It was an attitude that was evident in other graduates of the school from before the war, working around the globe – most notably Maxwell Fry. Fry's numerous large-scale projects undertaken with Jane Drew in Ghana, Mfantsipim School (1953, fig. 82), Mauritius Legislative Assembly Government Centre (fig. 83), together with their new capital city of

Fig. 83 Legislative Assembly Government Centre, Port Louis, Mauritius, 1970s, Edwin Maxwell Fry & Jane Drew.

British Architectural Photograph Library / Royal Institute of British Architects

Fig. 84 Government College for Women, sector 11, Chandigarh, 1950s, Fry, Drew, Knight & Creamer.

British Architectural Photograph Library / Royal Institute of British Architects

Chandigarh, Punjab (1950s, fig. 84) in collaboration with Le Corbusier and Pierre Jeanneret, demonstrate 'the possibility that Western architects may become acculturated to non-European idioms and continuously reinterpret Modernism in their terms'.[66] Their Co-operative Bank of Western Nigeria, Ibadan (1962, fig. 85), was undertaken in partnership with Drake and Denys Lasdun, while their AIA Building in Singapore from the 1960s was designed together with Knight & Creamer (fig. 86). Others such as Peter Shepheard would display a maverick tendency, as evidenced in his landscape designs for the Festival of Britain (1951, fig. 87). As Thistlewood notes, '[this] and his subsequent contributions to the theory and practice of landscape architecture are deeply picturesque – something normally eschewed by the Liverpool School in favour of the regular and purposive ... questioning whether the neo-Classical should necessarily give way to Modernism rather than neo-Romanticism'.[67] Shepheard continued to work against the general tide of Modernism when in 1955 he produced his award-winning low-rise housing scheme for the London County Council. Shepheard was a visiting professor at the University of Pennsylvania in 1957 and in 1971 became professor there with tenure, where he remained until 1994. During the course of his career he wrote numerous books on landscape design and some of his most famous projects include work at London Zoo, Bessborough Gardens and the gardens of the US Ambassador at Winifred House. In 1972 he was awarded a CBE and was knighted in 1980. Shepheard was President of the Landscape Institute from 1965–66 and awarded the Landscape Institute Medal (UK), the profession's highest accolade, in 1999.

Robert Gardner-Medwin reflected this attitude when he returned to his alma mater as Roscoe Professor where he encouraged a generation of students to gain work experience overseas during the course of their training, developing Liverpool's long tradition of drawing students from around the globe. With Gardner-Medwin's encouragement Frank Jones established an important post-graduate programme of studies for overseas students. The new Professor was assisted in his endeavours by a talented group of colleagues teaching in the school – most eminent of these was Colin Rowe. Rowe achieved his Royal Gold Medal on the basis of his writing and educational achievements. In books such as *Collage City* (with Fred Koetter, 1978) and *The Architecture of Good Intentions* (1994) he helped liberate the architectural debate from the historicist language in which it had so often been conducted. In the process he also freed it 'from the mechanisms of opposition and alternative which have conventionally ruled stylistic debate ... he ... proposed criteria based upon intentionality, and an evaluative terminology reflective of practitioner concepts – light, texture, substance, posture, the collaging of planned and unplanned, the weaving together of old and new – as the means of reclaiming architectural debate from ideologues'.[68] Another innovation established by Gardner-Medwin was the first serious study of housing problems conducted within the school, funded by the Rowntree Trust. The school had a long interest in social housing established in the Reilly era and continued via the many graduates who headed numerous City Architect and Town Planning Departments. Another was the appointment of a sociologist – Frank Horton – to the school's staff, reflecting the then growing acknowledgement of the importance of the sociological impact of architectural design. The wartime link with Poland was revived during this time and a number of exchanges took place, while another former student of the school who had returned to teach, Quentin Hughes (B.Arch. 1947, Dip.CD, MA), was seconded from the school to establish a new department of architecture in Malta with a number of his colleagues teaching there throughout the 1960s and 1970s. Hughes went on to write a number of seminal works on the architecture of Liverpool notably *Seaport: Architecture and Townscape*

Fig. 85 Co-operative Bank of Western Nigeria, Ibadan, 1962, Edwin Maxwell Fry, Jane Drew, Denys Lasdun & Drake.

British Architectural Photograph Library / Royal British Institute of Architects

Fig. 86 AIA Building, Singapore, 1960s, Fry, Drew, Knight & Creamer.

British Architectural Photograph Library / Royal Institute of British Architects

Fig. 87 Festival of Britain, Downstream Piazza with Homes and Gardens Pavilion on the right, South Bank, London, 1951, Peter Shepheard (landscaping and piazza).

British Architectural Photograph Library / Royal Institute of British Architects

Fig. 88 *Woman's Journal* 'House of the Year', Beaconsfield Road, Liverpool, 1960, Gerald Beech and Dewi Prys Thomas. The house consists of ground floor brick elevation with white Tyrolean finish, while the upper storey is timber framed and clad forming a cantilevered box. The openings are carefully placed and well proportioned with the greatest of care for both the internal and external effect. The garden with its reflecting pool, adjusted ground levels and planting was an integral part of the design.

The University of Liverpool, Library

in Liverpool (1964). Similarly Carl Pinfold, who originated from South Africa, was seconded to the University of Nairobi for three years to act as advisor on the development of its course in architecture. Other distinguished teachers from this period include Dewi-Prys Thomas and Gerald Beech (B.Arch.1947) whose collaborative design won the *Woman's Journal* 'House of the Year' competition in the early 1960s, for a house in Woolton, Liverpool (fig. 88).

Gardner-Medwin's tenure in the Roscoe Chair coincided with the major expansion of the British university system in the 1960s. Liverpool University undertook a large building programme to accommodate the increase in students and a number of graduates of the school were commissioned to design buildings for the university. An early example is Gordon Stephenson's design for the new building to house the Department of Civic Design (1950–52, fig. 89), where he had recently been appointed the Lever Professor in succession to

William Holford. Other examples include Maxwell Fry's Civil Engineering (1959) and Veterinary School (1960) buildings; Gerald Beech's Pavilion, Wyncote (1961–62, fig. 90), where the purist influence of the Bauhaus is displayed in the elegant design which won him a Civic Trust National Award; Peter Shepheard's extension to the Student Union (1961–63); Tom Mellor's (B.Arch. 1938, Dip. Civic Design 1938) Senate House (1967–68) and Gardner-Medwin's own designs for the university science lecture halls from 1967. Gardner-Medwin also designed a major extension to the Engineering Building at Edinburgh University on which he collaborated with three of his best recent graduates, James O'Donohue (B.Arch.1957), Devaprosad Chakravarti (B.Arch. 1956) and Stuart Russell (B.Arch.1956). Other smaller works of significance undertaken by graduates for the university include designs by Ken Martin (B.Arch.1961). Martin has gone on to combine a successful career as an academic with a professional practice – he was Head of the

Fig. 89 Department of Civic Design, Bedford Street, Liverpool University, 1950–51, Gordon Stephenson. Stephenson had returned to Liverpool when he was appointed Lever Professor. The building he designed for the department was part of the post-war redevelopment of the university and an early breakthrough into the modern style. Stephenson is reported to have designed it over the course of a weekend! Quentin Hughes notes of the building 'The main block has a well handled relationship of solid to void, but its link to the criticism room on the side elevation is clumsy' (*Liverpool*, Studio Vista, 1969, p.130).

Robert Kronenburg

Fig. 90 Wyncote Sports Centre, Mather Avenue, Liverpool, 1961–62, Gerald Beech. This pavilion is a glass box cantilevered at first and second floor level, then pinched in above to form a wide viewing terrace covered by a wide flat roof that lines up with the surface of the glass box. The building sits like 'a Japanese temple, in a related setting of trees and grass' (Hughes, *Liverpool*, Studio Vista, 1969, p.111) The building won a Civic Trust Award.

The University of Liverpool, Library

67

Fig. 91 Playhouse Theatre (Extension),
Williamson Square, Liverpool, 1966–68,
Hall, O'Donahue & Wilson.

Robert Kronenburg

Department of the Built Environment at Liverpool Polytechnic (Liverpool John Moores University) for many years. He has undertaken work in the city and beyond, such as his conversion of the former Midland Railway goods warehouse for the conservation studios of the National Museums and Galleries on Merseyside, c.1995, and his rooftop extension to the nineteenth-century Melbourne Buildings, North John Street (1975). Martin also worked with Hall, O'Donahue and Wilson on what is one of the most successful buildings to be constructed in Liverpool city centre in the 1960s – the extension to the Playhouse Theatre (1966–68, fig. 91). As Quentin Hughes noted of the design 'This theatre extension both compliments the existing façade and stands as a work of architecture in its own right.'[69] Recent work undertaken by Martin includes a design for a new Floral Pavilion for New Brighton, Wirral (figs. 92, 93). Other students from Gardner-Medwin's era who have built in the city include Peter Carmichael (B.Arch 1965, MCD 1966) and Susan Carmichael (B.Arch 1965, MCD 1968), who in the early 1980s won the competition for the housing and landscape design of the Anglican Cathedral precinct as

well as their multi-award-winning work on the conversion of the Albert Dock warehouse complex. Part of the Albert Dock complex houses the Merseyside Maritime Museum, which was given a Civic Trust Award in 1987 and a RIBA Regional Award in 1988. The practice of Brock Carmichael, founded in 1974 – of which Peter was a partner and Sue a highly active consultant – has built extensively across all building sectors for a wide variety of clients both locally and nationally. The many awards they have won include a RIBA Award Commendation in 1987 for Claverton Court – a sheltered accommodation scheme in a conservation area – which also won a RIBA / DoE / NHBC Housing Design Award in 1985 and a Civic Trust Commendation in 1986. Riverside Walk, Preston, 1986, was also awarded a Civic Trust Commendation while their Woodchurch Action Plan, Birkenhead, won the John Coaker Award (Royal Town Planning Institute, North West Region) in 1985.

Beyond the university and city, the school's graduates continued to work on major projects in Britain and around the globe. John Whalley (B.Arch. 1956, M. Civic Design 1957) established an international career as a

Fig. 92 Floral Pavilion, New Brighton, Wirral, Merseyside, Ken Martin.

Ken Martin Architects

Fig. 93 Rooftop extension to the nineteenth-century Melbourne Buildings, North John Street, Liverpool, 1975, Ken Martin in partnership with Paul Unsworth.

Robert Kronenburg

69

Fig. 94 Photograph of Model of Redevelopment Scheme surrounding St Paul's Cathedral, London, 1956, William Holford.

The University of Liverpool, Archives

Fig. 95 Replanning Scheme for Piccadilly, London, 1962, William Holford.

The University of Liverpool, Archives

Fig. 96 Branch of Barclay's Bank, Maidstone, 1960, William Holford. A design that incorporates stylistic elements drawn from the Italian Renaissance, Art Deco and Jazz Modern to form an amalgam that has been identified by some commentators as being presciently post-modern in its conception.

landscape architect designing widely in Britain, France and Japan. He won the Reilly Medal in 1956 and was President of the Landscape Institute (PPLI) from 1985–87. Whalley's work includes Everton Park, Liverpool (1st Prize Winner 1967) and Liverpool International Garden Festival (1st Prize Winner 1982) which won a BALI Award of Merit in 1984 and a Civic Trust Award in 1985. Other Civic Trust Awards were achieved for his work on the Cheshire Constabulary HQ (1969) and the Royal Life Offices, Peterborough (1992) to name but two. On an international level, Whalley is the designer of Urban Park, Cergy-Pntoise (1970) and, in collaboration with Allain Provost, La Courneuve Regional Park, Paris (1972). Vic Basil (B.Arch. 1956) was Chair of Lord Holford's offices in Liverpool and Manchester following Holford's sudden death in 1975 and designed numerous buildings including the Atlantic Tower Hotel, Pier Head, Liverpool (1973). His partner John Pickles (B.Arch. 1961) was a fellow graduate whose work on the restoration of Liverpool's Albert Dock received the highest European Conservation Award. Ronald Hancock (B.Arch. 1956, M. Civic Design 1957) was a senior partner in the firm of KKA and a former President of the Liverpool Architectural Society. Following a period working in the USA, he returned to teach in the school. Hancock's work includes numerous urban renewal housing schemes, including Wapping and Waterloo Docks, Liverpool, as well as schemes such as the Corner Project for Royal Insurance on Old Hall Street, Liverpool. Maxwell Fry's work in Africa and India has already been mentioned as has James Stirling's and Gordon Stephenson's. William Holford, while Lever Professor, produced a development plan for Liverpool University in 1949 – this provided the prototype for future university campuses he would later design. After vacating the Lever Chair, Holford accepted the commission to undertake a study of the development of the bombed area around St Paul's Cathedral (1956, fig. 94). He went on to develop other schemes such as his 'double-decker' proposal for Piccadilly (1962, fig. 95) – although this scheme was finally not implemented – as well as projects overseas such as his work on the planning of the Australian capital city, Canberra. Holford also collaborated with Mies van der Rohe on proposals for the Mansion House site, London, and with Oscar Niemeyer when he was consultant to Brasilia, 1957. In 1960 Holford designed a branch of Barclay's Bank in Maidstone, Kent (fig. 96), combining references to the Italian Renaissance, Art Deco and Jazz Moderne – a

71

Fig. 97 Quay Bar, Castlefields, Manchester, Stephenson Bell.

Stephenson Bell, Architects

design Thistlewood detected as being presciently post-modern in its conception when he noted that the building 'ought to figure in the cultural interpretations of such as Robert Venturi and Charles Jencks'.[70] Holford was Professor of Town and Country Planning at University College London from 1948 until his retirement in 1970, President of RTPI from 1953–54, and of RIBA from 1960–62. In 1963 he was awarded the RIBA Gold Medal; he was knighted in 1953 and in 1965 made a life peer, becoming the first town-planner to be honoured in this manner.

Roger Stephenson OBE (B.Arch.1969) is the director of Stephenson Bell, a nationally acclaimed practice based in Manchester which he co-founded in 1979. Stephenson has been awarded over 40 national awards for his designs including being shortlisted for the Stirling Prize in 1998 for Quay Bar, Castlefield, Manchester (fig. 97) which also won a RIBA Award. Other schemes that have been recognized by RIBA Awards include Deansgate Quay, Manchester in 2001 (fig. 98); and Astra Zeneca, 2006 (fig. 99). Following the 1996 IRA bombing of Manchester city centre, Stephenson's firm has played a major role in the rebuilding of the city, including projects such as Dukes 92 (fig. 100) and Chorlton Park. Many of these projects involve historic buildings, finding new uses for them that work within the historical context of the city. Stephenson holds a number of external positions including chairman of Manchester City Council's Conservation Areas and Historic Buildings panel. He is a visiting professor and external examiner at the Chinese University, Hong Kong as well as acting as an external examiner at Newcastle University. Other positions include acting as a jury chairman for the RIBA Awards; he is also a RIBA national councillor.

THE MODERN SCHOOL (1973–PRESENT)

When Gardner-Medwin retired in 1973, it brought to an end a forty-year period during which the Roscoe Chair had been occupied by ex-students of the school. Whereas previously many of the teaching posts had been held by Liverpool graduates, as the school gradually became more research orientated, fewer former students were employed after graduation. His successor, Professor John Tarn, inherited a school that would, in common with the broader university sector, face a period of great change and turbulence combined

Fig. 98 Deansgate Quay, Manchester, Stephenson Bell.

Stephenson Bell, Architects

Fig. 99 Astra Zeneca, Alderley Park, Cheshire, Stephenson Bell.

Stephenson Bell, Architects

Fig. 100 Dukes 92, Manchester, Stephenson Bell.

Stephenson Bell, Architects

Fig. 101 New Studios and Exhibition Space, School of Architecture, Liverpool University, King McAllister.

Martin Winchester

Fig. 102 Battersea Park Boat House, London, Rod McAllister.

Rod McAllister

Fig. 103 Concert Square, Liverpool, ShedKM for Urban Splash. This was the first of the urban regeneration schemes in what became known as Liverpool's Ropewalks district. The district is now home to a mix of apartments, restaurants, bars, shops and galleries.

Urban Splash

with financial restraints that required a good deal of resourceful planning in order for them to be overcome. In the mid-1980s, a merger of the School of Architecture with the Department of Building Engineering was set up in the Faculty of Social and Environmental Studies, offering courses recognized by both RIBA and CIOB. The consequences of the merger was that over £1 million of building investment was brought into the new School of Architecture and Building Engineering, allowing for a virtual rebuild of the old Budden building in order to create much needed new studio space, laboratories and an exhibition gallery (fig. 101). The scheme was undertaken by Dave King and Liverpool graduate Rod McAllister (B.Arch. 1987), winning a RIBA Award in 1989. Other schemes undertaken by the practice of King McAllister for the university include a design for the Student Services' Centre which won a RIBA Award in 1995. McAllister has designed numerous buildings in Britain and abroad that have received major awards, including the masterplan for the University of Perpignan, France – winner of the International Union of Architects'

Jeune Architects Grand Prix, 1992; Mellangoose, Falmouth – RIBA Award 1999; Battersea Park Boat House (fig. 102) – Building of the Year Award & Fine Arts Commission Trust 2002, and Battersea Park Pump House, Civic Trust Commission, 2006. His latest work for the university includes a major extension to the School of Tropical Medicine, together with a remodelling of the Department of Electrical Engineering. McAllister has been a partner of Sheppard Robson, London since 2003, as well as being a visiting professor at University of Rome, La Sapienza.

The architectural firm of ShedKM, which King and McAllister co-founded, has also been responsible for producing a number of projects for the development firm of Urban Splash, which was co-founded in the 1990s by Tom Bloxham and the Liverpool School of Architecture graduate, Jonathan Falkingham (BA 1984, B.Arch. 1988). Urban Splash specializes in the regeneration of derelict urban spaces – often difficult sites that other developers have been reluctant to tackle. Their earliest scheme was Concert Square (fig. 103), a development in Liverpool involving the conversion of an old factory and warehouses into apartments and bars, surrounding a newly designed city centre square. Numerous other schemes followed in Liverpool, Manchester, Sheffield, Bradford, Birmingham and Plymouth. Many of the schemes have won awards for their imaginative use of formerly redundant buildings in the Ropewalks and Castlefield districts of Liverpool and Manchester. The Urban Splash, ShedKM collaboration on the Manchester Moho (short for modular housing) scheme (figs. 104, 105) is perhaps one of their most exciting developments. Aimed at recent graduates and key workers, allowing them to afford to buy in the city centre where previously they had been priced out of the market, ShedKM's solution turns the standard model for prefabricated units on its head. Whereas prefab apartments are usually a series of rooms built separately in a factory and joined together on site, the Moho apartments are built fully formed in the factory and transported and installed on a six-storey prefabricated steel frame, saving six months in the construction process. In 2006, Urban Splash undertook the development of two Birmingham landmarks: the Rotunda and Fort Dunlop (fig. 106) – and in 2008 redeveloped the Oliver Hill designed art deco Midland Hotel in Morecambe.

Jim Eyre OBE (BA 1980) partner in the firm of Wilkinson Eyre, has achieved an international reputation for the quality of its work around the globe. The firm's position in the top league of architectural practices was cemented when they became the only practice to win the Stirling Prize twice, in 2001 for the Magma Science Centre, Rotherham, and in 2002 for their Gateshead

Fig. 104 Moho, Manchester, ShedKM for Urban Splash.
Urban Splash

Fig. 105 Moho, Manchester, ShedKM for Urban Splash.
Urban Splash

Fig. 106 Fort Dunlop, Birmingham, ShedKM for Urban Splash.
Urban Splash

Fig. 107 Gateshead Millennium Bridge, 2001, Wilkinson Eyre.
Wilkinson Eyre Architects

Millennium Bridge design (figs. 107, 108). When he formed his practice with Chris Wilkinson, the firm's early reputation was based on large long-span, low-cost structures. Groundbreaking bridge designs from the mid-1990s onward became something of a specialism of the practice which Wilkinson describes as having 'started with winning the first competition run by the London Docklands Development Corporation for a bridge over South Quay near Canary Wharf. Not many architects were involved with bridges then and the Docklands Development Corporation was looking for a practice which could turn its hands to them.'[71] This culminated in the Gateshead Millennium Bridge, which consists of two graceful curves, one forming the deck and the other supporting it, spanning between two new islands that run parallel to the quayside. Pivoting around their common springing points using an innovative rotational movement that has been likened to a slowly opening eye-lid, they allow shipping to pass beneath. Other award-winning designs by the firm include a Stirling Prize shortlisting for Stratford Regional Station in 1999 – the station won numerous prizes including RIBA and Civic Trust Awards. Liverpool Arena and Convention Centre (fig. 109), on the King's waterfront, which opened in 2008, forms the focal point of the city's European Capital of Culture celebrations, expressing its many functions in a series of unified forms that relate to its neighbours on the Liverpool waterfront. Following an international competition, Wilkinson Eyre was selected to design a 437.5m tower in Guangzhou (fig. 110). This mixed use development, consisting of offices and a hotel, when completed in 2010 will become one of China's tallest buildings, and the fourth tallest in the world.

Michael Stacey (BA 1980, B.Arch. 1984) continues the school's long tradition of producing graduates who combine successful academic careers with professional practice. In 1987 Stacey co-founded the firm of Brookes Stacey Randall Architects – a multi-award-winning

Fig. 108 Gateshead Millennium Bridge, 2001, Wilkinson Eyre.
Wilkinson Eyre Architects

Fig. 109 Liverpool Arena and Conference Centre, King's Waterfront, 2008, Wilkinson Eyre.
Wilkinson Eyre Architects

Fig. 110 Guangzhou West Tower, China, completion due 2010, Wilkinson Eyre.
Wilkinson Eyre Architects

Fig. 111 Boat Pavilion, Streatley-on-Thames, 1997, Michael Stacey.

Michael Stacey

practice. His Boat Pavilion, Streatley-on-Thames from 1997 (figs. 111, 112), won a RIBA Regional Award. Built on a sensitive site in rural Berkshire, previous designs had been rejected by planners on the grounds of being too intrusive. Stacey's solution was to create a glass enclosure, which provided superb views while also leaving the riverbank uninterrupted by virtue of its transparency. Drawing as it does upon the precedents of Mies van der Rohe, Phillip Johnson and Charles Eames, Stacey notes of the design 'I believe the Boathouse has achieved that rare quality that it appears to always have belonged in this landscape. Architecture is more than packaging; in a confusing world littered with ephemera it can provide an authentic voice.'[72] In 2003 Stacey, along with Nik Randall, left the practice to pursue independent careers. Stacey continues to combine practice, research, writing and teaching; he is the author of *Component Design* and the inventor of the Aspect 2 integrated composite cladding system, marketed by Corus. He

holds a chair at Nottingham University, and is a Visiting Professor at the University of Waterloo, Ontario.

Throughout the 1980s and 1990s, the school continued to produce graduates who would go on to build around the world gaining national and international awards for their designs. Jonathan Ellis-Miller's (BA 1983, B.Arch. 1986) design for a house for himself in 1991, built shortly after graduation, is set in the village of Prickwillow, Cambridgeshire, looking out onto a rural landscape with views of Ely Cathedral (fig. 113). As Neil Jackson notes of the house, 'Ellis-Miller's own studio house was a homage to the lightweight Case Study Houses of Raphael Soriano and Craig Ellwood ...'[73] The entire shell was pre-fabricated and as Ellis-Miller notes of the construction method employed, 'I had to use a method of construction that allowed me to use my time in the best possible way. It helped me create a really beautiful house for just £40,000.'[74] The house won Ellis-Miller a RIBA British Steel Award in

Fig. 112 Boat Pavilion, Streatley-on-Thames, 1997, Michael Stacey.

Michael Stacey

Fig. 113 Ellis-Miller House, Prickwillow, Cambridgeshire, 1991, Jonathan Ellis-Miller.

Ellis-Miller Architects Designers

Fig. 114 Banham Studio House, Cambridgeshire, Jonathan Ellis-Miller. *Ellis-Miller Architects Designers*

1993. When the painter Mary Banham was looking for a studio near Cambridge, the plot next to Ellis-Miller's own house was available. Ellis-Miller designed a house for Banham that complements his earlier design, and demonstrated the maturity he had gained as an architect in the intervening years. As Jackson notes of the Banham House (fig. 114)

> The bolted steelwork is bold, the cantilevers are deep and the scale is considerably inflated. But the houses are turned at right angles to each other and kept as far apart as the site will allow, thus reducing the contrast. Moreover, the application of a cantilevered steel access deck, overhead louvers and broad, Venetian blinds to the exterior of the Banham House serves to emphasise the horizontal and give the building the appearance of hovering Farnsworth-like, over its site.[75]

Ellis-Miller has designed numerous other award-winning buildings and is the recipient of seven RIBA awards, to date. His firm has recently been appointed by LendLease Projects to provide masterplanning and architectural design services on a £26m urban re-development of Oakham, Rutland.

Charlie Hussey (BA 1983) is the co-founder with Charlie Sutherland of the practice of Sutherland Hussey. In 1987 Hussey joined the office of Sir James Stirling, leaving in 1994 to work briefly with Renzo Piano in Italy, before returning to Scotland in 1997 to set up practice. Since then the firm has completed a wide range of projects including private residences such as The Barnhouse, Highgate (fig. 115), which was awarded the AJ First Building Award at the 2002 Stirling Prize ceremony. Other schemes include an Art Gallery in Inverness and Lynher Dairy, Cornwall (fig. 116), which won both RIBA and Civic Trust Awards in 2003. Their designs for an arts project – An Turas

Fig. 115 The Barnhouse (interior), Highgate, Charlie Sutherland & Charlie Hussey.

Sutherland Hussey Architects

Fig. 116 Lynher Dairy, Cornwall, Charlie Sutherland & Charlie Hussey.

Sutherland Hussey Architects

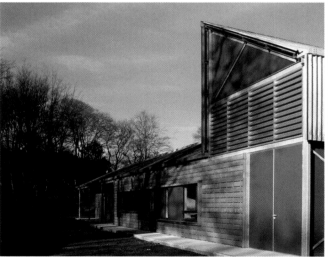

Fig. 117 An Turas (The Journey), Tiree, Charlie Sutherland & Charlie Hussey.
Sutherland Hussey Architects

(The Journey) – Tiree (figs. 117, 118), was awarded the RSA Gold Medal, a RIBA Regional Award, as well as being shortlisted for both the RIAS Architecture Award and the Stirling Prize, in 2003. In 2006 the Tiree design was one of six buildings selected by Royal Mail to appear on a set of stamps issued to celebrate contemporary British architecture. The ethos of the practice is one of diversity rather than specialism with the approach to each design problem taking on an almost empirical objectivity. The elimination of preconceived ideas helps to highlight the creative potential of each project and site such as in their design for a Boat House, Lower Mill Estate, Gloucestershire, which was exhibited at RIBA and the V&A in 2005. Their latest commission is to design the Chengdu Museum, China. This £240 million contract was won by beating off competition from practices in France and China, and when completed will occupy a full square in the centre of the city of Chengdu, Capital of the Sechuan Province.

Simon Henley (BA 1989), co-founder in 1995 of the firm of Buschow Henley, has undertaken a broad range of work in housing, healthcare, office design, urban regeneration and masterplanning. In addition to new-build work, their portfolio includes work on the adaptive reuse of historic buildings. The practice has won numerous national and international awards, including a RIBA Award for the Shepherdess Walk mixed-use building in 2000 (fig. 119); the design for offices and studios for TalkBack Thames (2002,

Fig. 118 An Turas (The Journey), Tiree, Charlie Sutherland & Charlie Hussey.
Sutherland Hussey Architects

Fig. 119 Shepherdess Walk, mixed-use development, London, 2000, Simon Henley.
Buschow Henley

85

Fig. 120 TalkBack
Thames, offices, London,
2002, Simon Henley.
Buschow Henley

figs. 120, 121), was judged by the German journal *AIT* to be one of the best new office buildings in Europe in 2004; a Housing Design Award for York Place in Leeds (2003); and an AIA / UK Excellence in Design Award Commendation for the St John's Therapy Centre (2007, fig. 122). In 2000 Buschow Henley was shortlisted for Building 'Young Practice of the Year' and in 2002 Henley was shortlisted for Corus 'Young Architect of the Year'. The firm's major competition wins include the regeneration of Chatham's historic Royal Dockyards, St Mary's Island, Kent (2001), Caldicott School Performing Arts Building (2001) and Bagby Airfield (2007). Buschow Henley was placed second in the DfES-sponsored Schoolworks Kingsdale School (2000), and IPPR's Designs on Democracy Letchworth Town Hall in 2003. Their work has been widely exhibited and published at the Ideal Home Show, RIBA, the Victoria & Albert Museum, London together with the Van Alen Institute in New York.

The firm of Lynch Architects – established by Patrick Lynch (BA 1990, B.Arch. 1993) and Claudia Lynch – has worked on a variety of different schemes, ranging from individual houses, residential and commercial developments, to arts and community projects. They explain their approach as being 'inspired by architecture that is a support for life and we seek to reveal in our work the latent historical continuity of places and human situations'.[76] This approach can be seen in designs such as the Madder Rose Gallery, East

Fig. 121 TalkBack Thames, offices, London, 2002, Simon Henley.
Buschow Henley

Fig. 122 St John's Therapy Centre, 2007, Buschow Henley.
Buschow Henley

Fig. 123 Madder Rose
Gallery, Whitecross St, East
London, 2007, Patrick Lynch.
Lynch Architects

Fig. 124 Madder Rose Gallery
(interior), Whitecross St, East
London, 2007, Patrick Lynch.
Lynch Architects

London (2007 figs. 123, 124) and Greenwood Road House, Hackney, London, built in 2006 (fig. 125). Of the latter design, Kieran Long notes that 'Lynch's house attempts to mediate the forms of the surrounding terraces with the lifestyle of a newer bourgeois culture – one that is entrepreneurial, not fixed to a single location and not bound by conventional class boundaries.'[77] The timber skin of the house is striated by timber batons on all four sides – the timber fascia is peeled away to create the opening for the balcony revealing the oak structure and views into the depth of the interior (fig. 126). As Long goes on to note

> Lynch Architects' work has an intellectually-imposing reputation, with buildings such as its Marsh View house … making statements on a small scale that attempt to deal with the spiritual as well as the worldly requirements of creating a dwelling. But the pleasure of the Hackney house is in its tangential relationship to its context. Here there is a wit and a certain freedom about Lynch's form making. As he himself says: 'I would rather my clients get more sunlight than to allow the typology to ossify or to be subservient to type. Form is the expression of freedom.'[78]

Prior to setting up in practice with Patrick, Claudia worked for many years in the offices of Michael Wilford & Partners and van Heyningen & Haward. Patrick Lynch has combined his practice with teaching, initially at Kingston University from 1997–2003, then at the Architectural Association from 2001–03; and London Metropolitan University 2005–07. Lynch Architects' projects have been widely published in the national and international media, and they were winners of the Young Architects of the Year Award, in 2005–06.

Any history such as this, spanning as it does over 100 years, will inevitably only be capable of mentioning a small proportion of the students who have passed through the school and made a name for themselves in the architectural world. While only a few can achieve the international acclaim of the likes of Maxwell Fry, Sir James Stirling, Colin Rowe or Lord Holford, it is nonetheless important to record and illustrate their achievements in order to demonstrate the enormous influence the school has had upon the architectural world for over 100 years. It is inevitable, however, that many talented graduates who have followed highly successful careers will be missed out from an account of this length and the people discussed are representative of the large number of graduates produced by the school throughout its long history. A number of graduates have established highly successful careers in other fields. Chris Lowe (BA 1981) has achieved international success as one half of the pop-duo, the Pet Shop Boys, selling more than 50 million records worldwide. Stephen Bayley (MA 1975) is the author of numerous books on the subjects of design and cultural history. In the 1980s he set up the Boilerhouse Project with Sir Terence Conran at the V&A, where he curated a series of major exhibitions, before going on to become the first director of the Design Museum in London. In 1989 Bayley was made a Chevalier de L'Ordre des Arts et des Lettres, France's top artistic honour.

The centenary celebrations of the school's foundation, held in 1995, were shortly afterwards followed by the retirement of Professor John Tarn. His successor to the Roscoe Chair, Professor David Dunster, inherited a school with a healthy research and teaching profile. Long-standing members of staff such as Professor Simon Pepper continue the school's tradition of high-quality research and teaching. Professor Pepper was Head of Department on two occasions, the last being 2001–05, during which time he helped to reinvigorate the research base within the school. Professor Pepper has personally won a number of substantial research grants – he has also encouraged other members of staff to develop their research activity. As a result hundreds of thousands of pounds of research grants have been attracted to the school in recent years. His research interests incorporate military architecture in the Mediterranean, late Renaissance art, the history of high-rise housing in early twentieth-century Britain and the history, condition and refurbishment of the British library system. Professor Pepper has published widely and is currently in collaboration with the department of Art History, Reading and the Barbour Institute of Fine Arts, Birmingham, towards publishing the volume in the series *The Paper Museum of Cassiano dal Pozzo*. This is one of the great collections of drawings assembled by the seventeenth-century antiquarian, now held in Windsor Castle, the British Library and the College de France. His position as a member on the RIBA Research Committee has recently resulted in his appointment on the H30 sub-panel: Architecture and the Built Environment, of the RAE.

Professor Robert Kronenburg became Head of Department in 2005. Among his research interests is the means by which temporary, ephemeral and flexible buildings and events impact on the architectural environment – in order to clarify the important role that temporary, transportable and flexible buildings have to play in creating appropriate, economic, sustainable modern architecture. Other research interests include his examination of the urban environment through the medium of film. Professor Kronenburg is co-principal researcher at the City in Film research project in the school, as well as being director of the Transportable and Adaptable Architecture Research Unit and president of the Liverpool Architectural Society, 2007/08. He has published widely, including writing for the New York journal *2wice*, *Fabric Architecture* and *Architectural Design* and is the author of a number of books, the most recent being *Flexible: Architecture that Responds to Change*.

Liverpool School of Architecture continues to attract high-quality students from across the UK and from countries around the world. The international reputation established in the pre-war years by Reilly and strengthened by Budden, Gardner-Medwin and their successors has produced, in recent years, a number of young architects who have swiftly established award-winning national and international reputations for the quality of their work. In December 2007 the launch of the *Liverpool School of Architecture Journal* has provided a new forum for architectural discussion, showcasing the work taking place within the school – as well as projects undertaken by its many graduates. The school has research expertise in architectural history, film, complexity and building, sustainability and regeneration. The school's establishment of the Centre for Architecture and the Visual Arts, and its involvement with the India and the World research centre indicates its continuing outreach agenda. The large research grants and consultancies that members of the academic staff attract to the school each year – which help to inform and develop their teaching programmes – would seem to indicate that many more high-quality graduates will come out of the school in the next century of its life. Going out to build around the globe, these graduates will continue to cement he Liverpool School of Architecture's long-standing reputation as the 'World in One School'.

Peter Richmond

Fig. 125 Greenwood Road, Hackney, London, 2006, Patrick Lynch.
Lynch Architects

Fig. 126 Greenwood Road (interior), Hackney, London, Patrick Lynch.
Lynch Architects

Fig. 127 End of year student exhibition, Liverpool School of Architecture.
Robert Kronenburg

END NOTES

1 See Mary Bennett, *The Art Sheds 1894–1905*, catalogue to an exhibition held at the Walker Art Gallery, Liverpool, 1981, for a fuller account of the history of the School of Applied Arts and the artefacts produced by its students.

2 See Christopher Crouch, *Design Culture in Liverpool 1880–1914*, Liverpool, Liverpool University Press, 2002, for more on Simpson's role in establishing a classical / Beaux Arts base before Charles Reilly.

3 Frederick Moore Simpson, *The Scheme of Architectural Education*, Liverpool, Marples, 1895.

4 Crouch, *Design Culture in Liverpool*, p. 91.

5 Bennett, *The Art Sheds*.

6 Charles Herbert Reilly, *Scaffolding in the Sky*, London, Routledge, 1938, p. 71.

7 See Crouch, *Design Culture in Liverpool*; also Peter Richmond, *Marketing Modernisms: The Architecture and Influence of Charles Reilly*, Liverpool, Liverpool University Press, 2001.

8 Charles Herbert Reilly, 'Introduction', *The Liverpool Architectural Sketchbook*, Liverpool, Liverpool University Press, 1910, pp. 11–12.

9 Leonard Eaton, *American Architecture Comes of Age*, Cambridge, MA, MIT Press, 1972, p. 31.

10 Crouch, *Design Culture in Liverpool*, p. 124.

11 ibid, p. 122.

12 David Thistlewood, 'Liverpool School of Architecture: Centenary Review', *The Architects' Journal*, 11 May 1995, p. 61.

13 See E. Hubbard and M. Shippobottom, *A Guide to Port Sunlight Village*, Liverpool, Liverpool University Press, 1988.

14 The finances were from part of a libel action Lever won from the *Daily Mail* totalling £91,000.

15 Reilly, *Scaffolding in the Sky*, p.127.

16 The University of Liverpool, Faculty of Arts, Chair of Civic Design, Report to Senate, 20 March 1912, Vice Chancellor's Papers, Liverpool University Archives, Box 6B/3/7.

17 For a full account of Abercrombie's career see Gerald Dix, 'Patrick Abercrombie 1879–1957', in G. E. Cherry (ed.), *Pioneers in British Planning*, London, The Architectural Press, 1981, pp. 103–30.

18 Bradshaw had entered the school as 'lantern and studio boy' and eventually enrolled as a student in 1911 largely due to Reilly's encouragement. He would go on to be the First Secretary of the Royal Fine Art Commission, 1923 and was a lecturer in History of Architecture at the Architectural Association.

19 For example Srinivasarao Harti Laksminarasappa (born c. 1885, Madras, Cert. Arch. 1912, B.Arch 1921).

20 The school had occupied part of the Bluecoat Chambers which Lever had bought and allowed the school to use – however, following a falling out between Lever and the university, the school was forced to move to less favourable accommodation on the university campus – a former hospital in Ashton Street that would be dubbed 'Reilly's Cowsheds'.

21 The annual intake of students rose steadily under Reilly's stewardship, from eleven in 1904 to 48 in 1932; the number of local students as a proportion of the whole fell dramatically, while those from around the UK and overseas far outnumbered them by the time of Reilly's retirement. See Classification and General Statistics, Liverpool University Archive, Box P5097, for a fuller set of student statistics.

22 For example a list for session 1928/29 includes L. M. Hernandez (Panama), M. Riad (Egypt), C. Tulyananda (Siam), D. M. Cowin (South Africa), V. N. Prasad (India), E. L. F. de Soysa (Ceylon), O. F. Weerasinghe (Ceylon), among others; Liverpool University Archives, Box P5097.

23 Reilly, *Scaffolding in the Sky*, p. 121.

24 See Khalid Sultani, 'Architecture in Iraq between the Two World Wars 1920–1940', *International Magazine of Arab Culture*, 2/3, 1982, pp. 92–105; also Freya Stark, 'Built on Sand', in *Baghdad Sketches*, repr. The Marlboro Press, c.1992.

25 Reilly, *Scaffolding in the Sky*, p. 210.

26 Quoted by Lord Kinross in a letter to *The Times*, 3 September 1965.

27 Interview with Joseph Sharples 18 January 1996 – see Joseph Sharples (ed.), *Charles Reilly and the Liverpool School of Architecture 1904–1933*, Liverpool, Liverpool University Press, 1996, pp. 37–38.

28 C. H. Reilly, 'Some More Empire Banks', *The Banker*, February 1935, p. 274, quoted in Sharples (ed.), *Charles Reilly*, p. 38.

29 See C. H. Reilly, 'Architecture as a Career for Men and Women', *Journal of Careers*, March 1931.

30 L. Budden (ed.), *The Book of the Liverpool School of Architecture*, Liverpool, Liverpool University Press, 1932, p. 44; student record card, University of Liverpool Archives, Box A.240.

31 Lunn produced this design in his final year at the school; he had previously worked in the New York offices of Corbett, Harrison and MacMurray and the detailing of this, his thesis design, clearly shows the influence of the Art Deco detailing he saw on the skyscrapers there.

32 J. H. Forshaw, 'The Architectural Work of the Miners' Welfare Committee', *RIBA Journal*, 7 March 1938, p. 426.

33 Sharples (ed.), *Charles Reilly*, p. 29.

34 Information provided during an interview between J. S. Allen and Joseph Sharples, 28 February 1995, ibid, p. 30.

35 Reilly criticized the decision of the tunnel committee not to involve an architect earlier in the project, feeling that Rowse's designs had as a consequence been compromised and that Rowse had 'been set the impossible task of decorating what is really but a hole in the ground. The engineer too often feels he can cover up his mistakes by calling in an architect to add pretty things to hide them'; Reilly, *Liverpool Review*, August 1934, pp. 273–74.

36 *Daily Post Liverpool*, 19 May 1934, p. 6.

37 C. H. Reilly, *Representative British Architects of the Present Day*, London, Batsford, 1931, pp. 25–26. See also S. Pepper and M. Swenarton, 'Neo-Georgian Maison-type', *Architectural Review*, 168, 1980, pp. 87–92 for a discussion of the Liverpool School in promoting the neo-Georgian model for social housing.

38 Letter from Reilly to Minoprio, 10 December 1931, quoted in Sharples (ed.), *Charles Reilly*, p. 132.

39 Johnson-Marshall was an eighteen-year-old schoolboy travelling on a train to Manchester to attend an interview to study Civil Engineering, when he had a chance meeting. He recalled that 'a plump gentleman got into the compartment

wearing a black coat and broad-brimmed hat. This gentleman engaged him in discussion and persuaded him that architecture was his real mission, and that he should accompany him to Liverpool for an interview with the Professor, who was none other than the plump gentleman, Sir Charles Reilly.' Percy Johnson-Marshall, quoted in A. Saint, *Towards a Social Architecture: the Role of School-Building in Post-War England*, 1987, p. 241.

[40] Thistlewood, 'Liverpool School of Architecture: Centenary Review', p. 65.

[41] M. Wright, *Lord Leverhulme's Unknown Venture*, London, Hutchinson Banham, 1982, p. 65.

[42] D. Thistlewood, 'Liverpool School of Architecture: Centenary Review', p. 64.

[43] Robert Gardner-Medwin, 'Recollections of Sixty Years of Modern Architecture in Britain: 1930–1990', p. 12, unpublished memoirs, copy in Walker Art Gallery Archive, Charles Reilly and the Liverpool School of Architecture 1904–33, Box 4.

[44] S. C. Ramsey, 'Charles Herbert Reilly', in Budden (ed.), *The Book of the Liverpool School of Architecture*, pp. 27–28.

[45] W. J. R. Curtis, *Modern Architecture Since 1900*, London, Phaidon Press, 1996, pp. 335–36. For a fuller account of the background to the involvement of Reilly and Crabtree in the Peter Jones store's design, see Richmond, *Marketing Modernisms*, pp. 168–76.

[46] Sharples (ed.), *Charles Reilly*, pp. 32–33.

[47] N. Pevsner, *The Buildings of England: North Lancashire*, Harmondsworth, Penguin, 1969, p. 65.

[48] For more on Barman's career see Bruce Paget, 'An Evaluation of the Work of Christian Barman', unpublished undergraduate thesis, Trent Polytechnic, 1988, held in London Transport Museum Library.

[49] W. Holford, 'Sir Charles Reilly', *Architectural Review*, 103, May 1948, pp. 180–83.

[50] Gardner-Medwin, 'Recollections of Sixty Years of Modern Architecture in Britain', pp. 11–12.

[51] Quoted in Alan Powers, 'Liverpool and Architectural Education in the Early Twentieth Century', in Sharples (ed.), *Charles Reilly*, p. 17.

[52] Anthony Jackson, *The Politics of Architecture: A History of Modern Architecture in Britain*, London, The Architectural Press, 1970, p. 20.

[53] Wesley Dougill, 'Work of the Schools: Liverpool', *Architects' Journal*, 6 July 1932, p. 12.

[54] Thistlewood, 'Liverpool School of Architecture: Centenary Review', p. 62.

[55] E. Maxwell Fry, *Autobiographical Sketches*, London, Elek, 1975, p. 136.

[56] Thistlewood, 'Liverpool School of Architecture: Centenary Review', p. 63.

[57] Arthur Trystan Edwards wrote a series of articles for *Town Planning Review* in the period 1914–18, while he was serving in the Royal Navy. During the middle years of the 1930s he wrote a series of articles published in *The Builder* in which slum clearance and the relative merits of high-density and low-rise building were discussed, such as 'A Hundred New Towns for Britain', 18 October 1935, p. 690. Edwards was a highly original thinker who was often ahead of the general architectural and planning debates of the time. He was much respected by Reilly and it is interesting to speculate to what extent he influenced Reilly with regard to his former teacher's developing architectural stance.

[58] ibid.

[59] Professor Simon Pepper recalls being told in the early 1970s by Lucjan Pietka – one of the members of staff from the Polish School who remained in Liverpool as a member of the teaching staff after the end of the war – that many of the Polish students were serving in the armed forces or merchant marine and fitted their studies into periods of rest and recuperation between tours of duty.

[60] Boleslaw Szmidt, 'Polish School of Architecture in Liverpool', *Art Notes*, VIII, 1, 1944, pp. 2–3.

[61] Lionel Budden, 'Introduction', *The Polish School of Architecture 1942–1945*, Liverpool, 1945.

[62] Astragal, *Architects' Journal*, 14 March 1946, quoted in catalogue to *The Polish School of Architecture Exhibition*, n.d. circa 1945, University of Liverpool Archives, Box D808/3/4.

[63] Rob MacDonald, 'James Stirling: Education of an Architect 1924–1954', p. 34.

[64] MacDonald, quoted in draft notes for 'James Stirling: Education of an Architect 1924–1954', kindly supplied by the author.

[65] James Stirling, 'Reflections on the Beaux-Arts', *Architectural Design*, XLVIII, 11–12, 1978, p. 88.

[66] Thistlewood, 'Liverpool School of Architecture: Centenary Review', p. 65.

[67] ibid, p. 64.

[68] ibid.

[69] J. Quentin Hughes, *Liverpool*, London, Studio Vista, 1969, p. 135.

[70] Thistlewood, 'Liverpool School of Architecture: Centenary Review', p. 63.

[71] C. Wilkinson, 'Wilkinson tells a story', www.royalacademy.org.uk/architecture/interviews.

[72] M. Stacey, *Acadia*, 1998.

[73] Neil Jackson, 'Fenlands Case Study', *The Architectural Review*, 1 October, 1998.

[74] Ben Flanagan, 'Here's one I made earlier', *Observer*, 29 February 2004.

[75] Jackson, 'Fenlands Case Study'.

[76] http://www.lyncharchitects.co.uk/aboutus.html

[77] Kieran Long, 'Iconeye – Greenwood Road House', *Icon*, 034, April 2006.

[78] ibid.

SUGGESTED FURTHER READING

Bennett, Mary, *The Art Sheds 1894–1905*, Walker Art Gallery, Liverpool, 1981 (catalogue)

Budden, Lionel, 'Charles Reilly: An Appreciation', *RIBA Journal*, March 1948, pp. 212–13

Budden, Lionel (ed.), *The Book of the Liverpool School of Architecture*, Liverpool, Liverpool University Press, 1932

Campbell, Louise, 'A Call to Order: The Rome Prize and Early Twentieth Century British Architecture', *Architectural History*, 32, 1989, pp. 131–51

Cherry, Gordon E., *Pioneers in British Planning*, London, The Architectural Press, 1981

Cherry, Gordon E. & Penny Leith, *Holford: a study in architecture, planning and civic design*, London, Mansell, 1986

Crouch, Christopher, *Design Culture in Liverpool 1880–1914: The Origins of the Liverpool School of Architecture*, Liverpool, Liverpool University Press, 2002

Dickinson, Page L., 'Lawrence Wright and his Work', *Pencil Points*, May 1931, pp. 327–42

Fry, E. Maxwell, *Maxwell Fry: Autobiographical Sketches*, London, Elek, 1975

Hubbard, Edward and Michael Shippobottom, *A Guide to Port Sunlight Village*, Liverpool, Liverpool University Press, 1988

Hughes, J. Quentin, 'Before the Bauhaus: The Experiment at the Liverpool School of Architecture and Applied Arts', *Architectural History*, 25, 1982, p. 102

– *Liverpool*, London, Studio Vista, 1969

– *Seaport: Architecture and Townscape in Liverpool*, Liverpool, Bluecoat Press, repr. 1993

Kelly, Thomas, *For the Advancement of Learning: The University of Liverpool 1881–1981*, Liverpool, Liverpool University Press, 1981

Newbery, Frank, 'Liverpool's Flats 1919–1939: Policy and Design of Central Areas Redevelopment by the Liverpool Housing Department', B.Arch thesis, Liverpool University, 1980